MIND IS THE MASTER
MASTER THE MIND

My Journey of Healing Through

HYPNOTHERAPY, COUNSELLING & THOUGHT YOGA

Includes

11 INSPIRING CASE STUDIES

by

Dr. RITU NANDA

First Published in 2024

ISBN: 979-889415052-9

Distributed by: Notion Press, Amazon, Flipkart

With the divine blessings of my Guruji...

Dedicated to

The memory of my mother Mrs. Swaraj Loomba, my first teacher, whose life lessons are deeply etched in me.

My daughter Surbhi, the girl with a golden heart, who turns all my dreams into reality.

and

All who love me and believe in my work.

To the seeking mind...

To a more confident, happy and joyous you.

You can't add a new book if your library is full.

Let's create a lot of humble energy before we read this book.

"I am humble, I am ready to learn

I don't crib, I don't complain

I am humble,

I learn."

Foreword

When I first started teaching Psychology, I found it difficult—much harder than teaching specific papers in psychology to answer the concepts, myths and misconceptions surrounding hypnosis. How could I link these doubts together for the student? I felt a bit like I was presenting a limited explanation rather than an integrated set of principles and knowledge. Of course, what was difficult for me was harder still for my students.

Much later, as a practising psychologist, I realised that there is an inherently fascinating quality about the topic of hypnosis. How is it defined? How is it produced? How is its impact measured? How can it be explained? How can it be used? These are questions that require to be addressed. It is here that **Dr. Ritu Nanda's** book **'Mind is the Master, Master the Mind'** comes in very handy. Not only does it dispel several myths about hypnosis and hypnotherapy but does so with case studies that one can relate to.

A unique feature of this book is the explanation of often misunderstood concepts of counselling and psychotherapy. Dr. Nanda simplifies it beautifully for people who may not have a psychology background. The ease and precision with which complex psychological therapeutic concepts are explained could only come with training and experience, which she has acquired over a long period of time. An amazing feature of the book is the positive tone with which psychological problems are explained and managed, a rare feature in a book dealing with psychopathology.

'Mind is the Master, Master the Mind' is destined to become the companion of people interested in clinical hypnosis. It begins with thorough coverage of the material typically found in workshops on mental health and then moves to more advanced hypnotic therapeutic interventions. The reader will learn about both the empirical basis of hypnosis and the practical "how-to" techniques that are necessary to conduct hypnotic inductions, intervene with hypnotic suggestions, and pursue the highest levels of its practice.

Dr. Vinay Mishra

Psychologist, Professor of Psychology

Acknowledgements

With deepest gratitude, I wish to thank the Supreme Power for giving me the courage to write this book and guide me throughout this journey.

I sincerely thank all those people who have come into my life, who inspired, motivated and encouraged me to evolve continuously and become a better version of myself.

I am deeply grateful to all my Teachers and Mentors for enlightening me with their words of wisdom and guiding my academic and spiritual journey.

My sincere thanks to Dr. Rakesh Jain for introducing me to the powers of Hypnosis and Past Life Regression Therapy.

I express my earnest thanks and gratitude to Sajan Galani who gave me invaluable insights into the amazing world of Hypnosis and Hypnotherapy and its immense potential, helping me gain hands-on expertise in this incredible art and science.

I am deeply indebted and thankful to Dr. Nitin Shukla for the exclusive training he imparted to me to advance my learning in hypnotherapy and be a Certified Clinical Hypnotherapist and Teacher with California Hypnosis Institute, USA.

I extend my special and sincere thanks to Dr. Vinay Mishra for his continuous support and encouragement in my work of healing and transformation, and for taking out time to write a foreword for this book.

From the depth of my heart, I express my honest and genuine thanks to my friend and colleague, Monika, who at every step, sustained my will and determination, and helped me discover my potential.

My special thanks to my friend Rajiv Mishra for placing the seed in my mind to write a book and for his unwavering belief in me.

My gratitude and thanks to Jatin Gupta and Sweta Samota for equipping me with the tools to turn this book into a reality. Special thanks to Indu and Mitesh Khatri for their constant inspiration and for raising my bar to platinum standards.

I sincerely thank my friend and author Arun Prabhu, whose work has constantly motivated me.

I am thankful to Ravi Tewari for his continuous support in publishing this book. He helped me cover the last and most important mile; making this book reach its audience.

I express my heartfelt thanks and gratitude to my loving family, especially my husband Deepak for believing in me and providing immeasurable support throughout. I thank the loving children of my family, Namiet, Soni, Surbhi and Jasmerr, who are a constant source of joy to me. Special thanks to my uncle Mr. Krishan Kumar Loomba who has been more than a father figure to me and for his continued support in my life.

I am grateful to all my clients who placed their trust in me and allowed me to heal them, and in turn, made me learn invaluable lessons at every step.

I sincerely thank all my friends, colleagues and students who have been a constant source of joy and happiness. You help me celebrate life and live it to the fullest.

Above all, I thank the Universe for manifesting my most cherished dream and bringing it to reality.

Preface

I recollect meeting an astrologer at our house one day. Everyone asked about their future. When my turn came, a relative remarked, "What do *you* want to ask now? You are married and you have two children. Your life is complete." That got me thinking. Is this the only purpose of life, getting married and bearing children? I wanted to break free from this stereotyped thinking, and I started dreaming.

I dreamt regardless of the constraints of age and time, tirelessly worked to find my true purpose, and finally found my calling in the world of healing.

As I healed others, my life transformed. Doors miraculously opened, and I kept walking with the Divine hand over me, and over all who were getting healed through me.

Your life is not just about you. It is about how you touch other lives.

Somewhere along this beautiful journey of healing, of transformation, of miracles, of blessings, I started feeling a deep urge to share it all. This book is the result of that long-cherished dream.

The mind is a good servant, but a bad master.

When you were a child and you felt sad, your mom gave you chocolates. Now every time you feel sad, you want a bar of chocolate. You can reprogram your mind out of it. It is incredible when you can look at that chocolate and *choose* to take it or leave it. This is freedom from compulsions. This example is just a drop in the ocean of what the wonderful mind can achieve.

This book explores the infinite powers of the subconscious mind and the immense potential of hypnotherapy and past-life regression therapy as healing modalities.

The unique counselling concepts shared are simple, yet very effective and if practised, would go a long way in changing perspectives, promoting positivity and enhancing emotional immunity.

Hypnotherapy provides ways to unfold one's full potential, leading to long-lasting self-mastery for higher levels of achievement in various spheres – personal, professional, studies and sports. It enhances the quality of life by promoting mental fitness, improving relationships, and creating meditative awareness.

The altered states of consciousness can be used to bring transformational changes and do away with limiting beliefs, remove blocks and obstacles to your inner peace, success, joy and happiness and put you in a peak state of performance.

Suggestion is power. The subtle force of repeated suggestion overcomes our reason, acting directly on our emotions and our feelings, and finally penetrating to the very depths of our subconscious mind. It is the basic principle of all successful advertising, the continued and repeated suggestion that makes you believe that you 'need to buy' something. This book covers how we can use the power of suggestion to bring about positive changes by reprograming the subconscious mind under trance.

Consciously or unconsciously, we are responsible for our thoughts, hence we have the power to choose them. We can evolve to unimaginable heights by directing our mental processes towards positivity. This book touches upon the technique of Thought Yoga, which allows one to not just manage, but master thoughts.

The case studies shared in the book are my personal experiences and healing sessions with clients. They involve the use of powerful therapies like hypnotherapy, past life regression therapy, hypnodrama, and techniques of behaviour modification to promote desirable behaviours, alleviate pain and suffering, to heal and transform. Each case study provides invaluable insights into the amazing world of therapeutic healing.

Our subconscious mind is a storehouse of riches and whatever we require, can be drawn from it. At any juncture of life, if we feel that our thinking, feeling, or behaviour is not conducive to our growth, we can reprogram our subconscious mind and bring lasting changes in ourselves. One can use this power to manage stress, overcome obstacles and frustrations, enhance confidence and willpower, improve relationships and quality of life, experience inner and spiritual contentment and reach one's highest potential.

This book attempts to make the readers aware of the greatest power within their reach – *'The Power of the Subconscious Mind.'*

With love and light

Ritu Nanda

CONTENTS

The mind is a mirror that has a tendency to gather dust through stress and strife of everyday life. And this dust must not be allowed to remain. Better still, the dust should not generate, and if there is any, it must constantly be wiped out.

- J. Krishnamurthy

Chapter 1

DOWN MEMORY LANE

Ritu! Get Up! Some guests are over. Please leave that book and serve them tea and some snacks. Ruby is not at home. Stop being a bookworm now!" That was my mother imploring me to leave my book and serve some guests who had arrived unannounced at our house. Grudgingly I left my favourite Enid Blyton and proceeded to do the needful.

My elder sister Ruby usually did that. She was very fond of socializing and attending to guests. I was fond of reading books. In my free time, I would sit in my favourite corner of the house with loads of homemade *chikki*, a dessert made from peanuts and jaggery, which my mother used to make lovingly and read my precious books, happily munching, and hanging on to every word of the enchanting stories. Oh, it was pure bliss!

Time passed. I completed my graduation in science. My mother was very firm and determined that I would not sit at home idle and would enrol in a postgraduation course. I was six years old and my sister Ruby, was eight when we lost our father to brain haemorrhage. I have very faint memories of him. My mother used to wear white sarees and I longed to see her in a colourful saree. I often had dreams of her visiting my school, dressed in a saree which had bright colourful flowers all over. Maybe because I would watch other children's mothers wear colourful dresses and visit school to meet the teachers.

With the unwavering support of my grandparents and extended family, my mother brought us up with great love and care, looked after every little need and played the role which only a mother can. I will forever be grateful to her for her strong decisions and teachings, which had a huge impact on me throughout my life and played a great role in moulding my personality.

I never wanted to study medicine or do my postgraduation in any of the science subjects. We were three friends and together got ourselves enrolled in English literature for our postgraduation course.

"What is your name?" asked the English teacher on the first day of the class.

"Ritu." I replied.

"What, Ritu? I never heard such a name. Couldn't you ever change it to Rita?" She commented rudely. That did not go down well with me. I love my name. I took an instant dislike for the teacher and later for the subject.

Some comments made by teachers, positive or negative, can greatly impact one's mind and stay with you for a lifetime.

After one week of attending the English class, we realised that this was not our cup of tea. Shakespeare used to go over our heads and we would sit in the class disinterested. Good sense prevailed and we opted out of the course. After inquiring about other subjects, we stumbled upon a psychology class and attended it. The fact that psychology is a science got us really interested in the subject. We liked and understood what was taught in the class and finally decided to study psychology. That was a turning point in my life.

I was faring well in the subject, but by the end of the second year of the course my marriage got fixed, that too just before the final exam. Thankfully my mother and I were determined that I appear for the exams and complete my course. As luck would have it, the exams got postponed and I got married. Post-marriage, I eventually completed my post-graduation in Psychology.

As time passed, I enjoyed marital bliss, lots of kitty parties, shopping and cooking at home, feeling free. No studies, no exams. Life was good. I was blessed with two lovely children and got busy bringing them up. Off and on I used to get this feeling that I ought to be more productive in life. I dabbled in various things. I remember fondly, that I always wanted to see myself on television. One day, I went to *Doordarshan Kendra*, met the director there, without any prior appointment, and told him that I wanted to do something on television. Perhaps I could conduct an interview. He listened to me patiently and told me that if a suitable opportunity came up, he would surely contact me.

Two days later, I got a call from *Doordarshan Kendra*. It was from a program coordinator. He told me that I had to interview a famous personality, whom they were inviting for a talk. I couldn't believe that my simple effort had paid off so quickly. All I had to do was take the first step! I immediately said yes! It was like a dream come true. He shared all the details with me and I was super excited. As the date approached, I had butterflies in my stomach. I was nervous about how I would face the camera and take the interview. I had no prior experience in this field. But I had committed and I had to stick to it.

I gathered myself and reached well before the scheduled time on the decided date, to get comfortable with the environment and the questions. Finally, the interview went off well and I felt relieved and happy with my accomplishment. I had not shared this with my family. When the interview was to be telecast, I asked them to watch the *Doordarshan* channel on TV. My husband and children were taken aback! They were elated to watch me on TV. It is a great feeling to watch yourself on TV and I felt on top of the world!

After that many programs followed. I got an offer to host a cookery show, *'City Rasoi'* on a local channel. *'City Rasoi'* became the talk of the town and many ladies wanted to be a part of it to showcase their culinary skills. I started the first episode with my mother-in-law and have very fond memories of it. Soon after, I got another offer to host a show named *'Solar Rasoi'* for MP Urja Vikas Nigam, as they were promoting solar cookers and fireless cooking. Many episodes were telecast and the show was quite popular and well-appreciated.

A few months later, I got an offer from the BPL Group to become their official cookery expert for microwave ovens. I thereafter conducted many sessions on microwave cooking for BPL. I was soon approached by a handloom brand 'Mrignayani' to model for their *sarees*. I still cherish fond memories of it. I was satisfied and happy that I was finally doing something worthwhile in my life.

"Take the first step in faith. You don't have to see the whole staircase. Just take the first step."

- Dr. Martin Luther King, Jr

ACT BEFORE YOU THINK!

20 years passed. I gradually started feeling a void within...that something was missing. I would often remember my books and think fondly of my subject psychology. The feeling grew and persisted and I started feeling as if there was a vacuum in my life, which I desperately wanted to fill. I wanted to study further, do something worthwhile in my subject, and take up a career related to psychology. There was an uncanny feeling that I was meant for much more.

One blessed day, my friend Monica, much younger than me, called and told me that she had enrolled in M.Phil. in Clinical Psychology at the University. The prerequisite for enrolling in the course was a post-graduate degree in psychology. She told me there were few seats left and that I had only a day left to register for the course.

A whirl of thoughts clouded my mind. This was a two-year-long intensive course with regular college hours. After twenty long years, will I be able to study again? Will I be able to attend college and appear for my exams? What if I failed?

Countless thoughts, mostly negative, dominated my mind. But somewhere a distinct inner voice told me, "Do not let go of this opportunity. You wanted to do something. Now is the time. Register for the course. So what if you fail? At least you will not have any regrets in your life." The best part was that I never got time to think or ruminate much because of the constraint of the last date for registration. That proved as a blessing and I finally enrolled for the course.

We have often heard people tell us: "Think before you Act." I discovered that sometimes it is better to "Act before you Think."

Overthinking and too much analysis causes paralysis, disabling you and preventing you from taking suitable action. Action propels you towards progress and overthinking curtails it, leaving you feeling doubtful, incomplete and dissatisfied.

There was a voice inside me, nudging me, urging me to do something more than what I was already doing. And The Universe sent me a boat. Without knowing fully where the shore was, I took a leap of faith and hopped on!

"If you really want something, the whole universe conspires in helping you to achieve it."

- Paulo Coelho in 'The Alchemist'

WHEN THE STUDENT IS READY, THE TEACHER APPEARS

I really enjoyed studying this advanced course in Clinical Psychology. I was an eager learner. I used to go to college regularly, never missed my classes and willingly absorbed every word spoken by my teachers. I was ready for this course. It was as if some unseen power was behind me, motivating me to move ahead.

I had lost touch with my studies and student life. I studied with students half my age. The course also was an advanced one and it demanded hard work. I referred to many books, made notes, and learned them religiously. Most of my time was spent on studies. My loving family supported and motivated me. My daughter was studying in eleventh grade then and I was studying in the first-year of M.Phil in Clinical Psychology.

I must admit that it was not all smooth sailing. I had my phases of doubt and unknown anxiety regarding the future. I am deeply grateful to my dear family for their tremendous support during this period. I have fond and cherished memories of time spent in college. I shared a wonderful bond with my classmates, which helped me throughout. As we reached closer to completion of the first year, it was time for D-day, the exam.

I entered the examination hall with mixed feelings of stress, excitement, and apprehension. When I received the question paper, I felt dizzy. How will I write a three-hour-long exam? My hands were sweaty and my heart was racing. For a few moments, I felt like leaving everything and running out of the examination hall. I felt I had forgotten whatever I had learned and time stood still.

With sheer grit and determination, I started to write without thinking too much about my anxiety. Thoughts kept flowing and my pen translated them onto the answer sheets. My focus was on writing the answers. I wrote, wrote and wrote... and three hours passed. It was time to put the pen down. As I handed over my answer sheet to the invigilator, I heaved a sigh of relief. I was drained.

My perseverance and sustained passion helped me sail through those two years of hard work. In the second year of the course, we were exposed to various therapies in Clinical psychology and had to undergo lots of practical training, which provided the base for future practice. Every year, we had to visit the Institute of Mental Health and Hospital, Agra (*Agra Mansik Arogyashala*) for practical training in clinical psychology. That training was instrumental in attaining in-depth knowledge of the practical aspects of the course and paved the way for further learning and future healing.

My goal was difficult but not impossible. **We should never confuse difficulty with impossibility**, because if something is difficult to achieve, it does not mean it is impossible. We try to escape difficulties in life and use the word 'impossible' instead.

Time flew and before we realised it was time for final year exams. I was pleasantly surprised and overjoyed when the results were declared. I had topped my class in both the first and second year of the course. I finally got an M.Phil. in Clinical Psychology.

I dared to dream and I had finally achieved it. Now, I had a designation to my name. I was a Clinical Psychologist. It took me some time to absorb how it felt. My life took a wonderful turn and I finally embarked on the beautiful journey of healing and transforming lives. I had found a purpose and my true calling. There was no looking back.

"He who has a 'why' to live for can bear almost any 'how.'"

- Fredrich Nietzsche

Chapter 2

CLINICAL PSYCHOLOGY A NOBLE FIELD

Many people live their lives or episodes of their lives in suffering and desperation, unable to cope with the challenges that prove to be overwhelming. The noble field of Clinical Psychology is concerned with these difficulties of human adaptation and with finding ways to prevent or reverse them. A Clinical Psychologist is involved in the assessment, diagnosis, intervention, and prevention of mental illnesses.

Over years of practice as a Clinical Psychologist, I discovered that some concepts work at the very core of effective therapy. A proper understanding of these concepts lays the foundation stone for successful therapeutic interventions and eventual healing. Let's dive in.

'Mental illness' is a general term that refers collectively to all the diagnosable mental disorders. Mental disorders are broadly classified into two categories, neurosis, and psychosis. We have a range of neurotic disorders and psychotic disorders. An easy way to remember the difference is by relating the word **neurosis with being closer to normality**. Less severe mental disturbances like stress-related disorders, anxiety disorders, mood disorders (mild depression or mania), etc. can be categorized as neurotic disorders. These can be treated with various psychotherapies and counselling techniques.

Psychosis is a severe mental illness in which a person is unable to distinguish reality from fantasy. Disorders like schizophrenia, delusional disorders, major depressive disorder, and manic-depressive psychosis, to name a few, come in the category of psychotic disorders. For Psychotic disorders, treatment involves the use of antipsychotic drugs and it is given by a psychiatrist. Any attempt to treat psychotic disorders only by therapy and counselling is heading for failure in the treatment. When residual symptoms are left, then therapies and counselling play a major role.

Pharmacotherapy and Psychotherapy should go hand in hand and they should complement each other. A multidimensional approach to treatment is always desirable. **The goal of any treatment is to promote autonomy and independence in the client and free him or her of medicines and therapy.**

People often ask "Why do I have this disorder? What is the reason?" Simply put, every disorder or mental illness has three aspects: **Bio. Psycho. Social.**

Bio includes the biological factors contributing to the illness, like hereditary factors, brain functions, neurotransmitter functioning, etc. Psycho includes psychological factors like mental makeup, thoughts, feelings, and emotions. Social includes sociological factors like the family environment, the social environment, and the culture of the concerned person. All these factors interplay and may have a significant role in precipitating the disorder.

The boundaries defining normal and abnormal are quite blurred.

A person showing normal behaviour may resort to abnormal behaviour in a fit of anger or adverse circumstances. People diagnosed with mental illness may exhibit lengthy periods of normalcy. The challenge is that during times of stress and adversity, if one can keep behaviour under conscious control, it can be called normal.

We must not label a condition as a disorder. When the symptoms fulfil the approved diagnostic criteria and there is an impairment in the personal, social, and occupational functioning of the person suffering from the condition, only then can we diagnose it as a disorder and give it a name according to the standardized classifications.

PSYCHOTHERAPY: THE TALKING CURE

Psychotherapy, often called the 'talking cure,' may be described as a conversation with a therapeutic purpose. Psychological intervention is a method of inducing changes in a person's thoughts, feelings, and behaviour. Psychotherapy involves intervention in a professional setting. It involves the application of psychological techniques and various therapies to bring about desirable changes in the client.

What can be learned, can be unlearned.

No child is born with a mental disorder. Have we ever come across a depressed or anxious child or a negative or bad child being born? These are all learnt behaviours due to many stressful life events and other related factors. As most problems develop through learning, they can be undone through unlearning and relearning in psychotherapy.

The nature of the relationship or therapeutic alliance between the client and therapist greatly impacts the success of psychotherapy. An accepting, non-judgmental environment in which clients can discuss their innermost secrets, urges and disappointments is extremely important to create. An effective therapist is someone who can be accepting, non-judgmental, objective, insightful and professional, all at the same time. These lavish objectives may not fit all therapists all the time, but the general ability of the therapist to rise above their personal views and provide an atmosphere of confidentiality, understanding and warmth, teamed with professional skills, go a long way in defining the success of therapy.

I always feel therapy works wonders. It is easy to understand if we look at it this way. Suppose there is a piece of sweet. After some time, ants will come and surround it. If you remove the ants, they will come again after some time, and every time you remove the ants, they will again surround the sweet. To remove the ants, we must first remove the sweet. So, the ants may be thought to be the symptoms a person is suffering from and the sweet is the cause for the symptoms. Symptoms are an effect of the cause. Just treating the symptoms will not be effective, since they will reoccur if you do not try to find the root of the problem and treat the underlying cause.

Effective therapeutic intervention involves going to the very root of the problem and trying to figure out the cause from where the problem arose and then eliminating the cause to the maximum extent, thus alleviating the symptoms. This is why therapeutic intervention takes time and may require many sessions to heal significantly.

The Psychotherapist should not be thought of as a mechanic, locating and repairing defects in a machine. But as a gardener who removes weeds, provides light, nutrients, and moisture to facilitate the inherent growth potential that is present in each individual.

The Root

I start my treatment by taking a detailed case history of the client. Taking the case history helps to build rapport with the client and instils an atmosphere of trust and faith in the therapist's competence. The confidentiality assured to the client and the nonjudgmental attitude of the therapist go a long way in motivating them to share their life's journey without holding anything back. This helps the therapist in understanding the psyche of the client and delving deep into the history of present complaints.

The predisposing, precipitating, aggravating, maintaining and relieving factors are also assessed before the start of the therapy session.

Predisposing Factors – These include genetic endowment and the environment as well as physical, psychological, and social factors in infancy and early childhood.

Precipitating Factors – These are events that occur shortly before the onset of a disorder and appear to have induced it. They may be physical, psychological or social.

Aggravating Factors – These include situations or events that aggravate the intensity of the disorder.

Maintaining Factors – These factors prolong the course of a disorder after it has been provoked and are instrumental in maintaining it. It is particularly important to pay attention to these factors as they greatly help in the overall treatment.

Relieving Factors – These factors are of utmost importance since they provide relief from disabling symptoms, though maybe for a brief period. They may involve a hobby or the company of a particular person or some environment which the client finds favourable.

Family history and relevant information regarding the problem are taken from concerned family members and significant others.

The threads of human misery are woven so tightly into the fabric of personal and social relationships, that it is essential to explore relationships and family's involvement in the client's life.

There is no stigma attached to consulting a psychologist. Psychotherapy is not specifically for the mentally ill. It is not aimed at curing only psychological ailments. Rather, counselling and therapy can be viewed as a vehicle for helping people in general get much more out of life. We need to create this awareness.

What is the nature of human nature? Psychology attempts to answer this question.

Let's discuss some unique counselling concepts in the next chapter. These concepts are simple, yet powerful in changing perspectives and creating self-awareness, leading to desired transformations. They can be used effectively along with traditional counselling methods.

Chapter 3

UNIQUE COUNSELLING CONCEPTS

Before we discuss the unique counselling concepts, let's understand the nature of counselling.

What is Counselling?

Broadly speaking, Counselling is an interaction which:

- Occurs between two individuals – Counsellor and Client
- Takes place in a professional setting
- Is initiated and maintained to facilitate positive changes in the behaviour of the client.

Counselling is guidance or advice given to a person who is in need, by a professional, at a professional level and when asked for.

Role of Counselling

Counselling plays a major role in dealing with client's problems when given in the right manner and at the right time. The role of counselling is developmental, preventive, remedial and restorative.

- ***Developmental***
  - o   To increase abilities & motivation
  - o   To improve interpersonal competencies
  - o   To foster positive self-image

- ***Preventive***
  - o   To avoid the recurrence of the same/other problem

- ***Remedial***
  - o   To help clients overcome failures
  - o   To overcome the present state of problems (personal, mental, social, academic, behavioural, vocational, etc.)
  - o   To make them aware of their strengths

- ***Restorative***
  - o   To modify behaviour and promote desirable behaviour
  - o   To restore the original healthy condition

In addition to proven psychotherapies, I use some very effective and unique counselling concepts while dealing with my clients. These are simple yet powerful, and go a long way in changing perspectives and modifying mindset and behaviour. Let's discuss them.

THE 'BUT' TECHNIQUE

I always use this simple technique before I start with therapeutic intervention. After taking the case history of my clients, I ask them to give me one word that is most important to them. Many people come up with different words like family, career, friends, love, peace, freedom, health, and so on. Whichever word they quote, I tell them, "Of course, it is a very important word, and holds great significance in one's life. Now today I want you to make one more word very important for yourself and include it as an important word in your life. And that word is 'BUT.'

For example:

- I feel disturbed due to my present situation, **but** I will come out of it.
- I am depressed due to certain stressful life events, **but** I can overcome it.
- I am facing trouble in my relationships, **but** I can cope in a better manner.

I then ask my clients to use the BUT technique and tell themselves, "Whatever difficulties I'm facing at present, or have faced in the past, whatever disorder I'm suffering from, whatever my condition now, **BUT** I am going to come out of this situation."

"With this faith, and with this hope, we will start our therapy work." I tell them.

The 'BUT' technique instils instant faith in the client and the therapy is set to proceed on a positive note.

"Hope is the Rope that swings you through life."

- Anonymous

THE POWER OF 'I AM'

*Your identity starts with the words **'I AM'**.*

I - Intention

A - Attention

M - Manifestation

The moment we say 'I AM,' we have set the ball rolling on how we would wish to define ourselves. The concept of 'I AM' says, first have an 'Intention.' Then, start giving 'Attention' to your intention, which may require passion and hard work. In due course of time, your intention, when given the right attention, will lead to 'Manifestation'. This is a sure-shot formula to achieve your goals in life. When we say 'I AM,' there is always a blank space after those words.

I AM _____________________

It is up to us what we fill in the blank. We can fill it with positive words and thoughts like:

"I am will- powered, confident, positive, happy, peaceful and a successful personality."

In contrast, we can fill that blank space with thoughts or words like:

"I am good for nothing. I am never on time. I mostly fail in whatever I do. I am unlucky. I am sad and depressed."

Everything is energy. So are our thoughts. This energy goes out in the form of vibrations to the universe. For all our thoughts, whether positive or negative, the universe has only one answer and that is **YES! or THATASTU!** It is up to us what we ask from The Universe. The Universe will reflect back to you who you are. It will not give you what you want. Realize the Power of the words 'I AM.'

I am deeply impacted by wonderful work done in the field of 'The Law of Attraction' by renowned authors and healers like Louise Hay, Abraham Hicks, Rhonda Byrne and Robert Anthony. I use the concept of 'I AM' and The Law of Attraction in my therapeutic sessions, thus motivating my clients to have a positive dialogue with themselves. This has brought transformational changes in my clients.

"The vibrations of mental forces are the finest and consequently the most powerful in existence."

- Charles Haanel

WHAT GETS ATTENTION GROWS

I have worked extensively as a Consultant Psychologist and Counsellor with many prestigious institutions, including schools and colleges, having spent over twenty glorious years with school children, working and solving various issues faced by them, by adolescents, parents, and teachers.

As I look back on this wonderful journey as a school counsellor, my heart swells up with cherished memories of innocent and sometimes anxious faces turning into smiling and relieved faces when simple efforts taken with love, care, and patience, solved their problems. Working with school children gave me wonderful insights into how the mind works, and what mistakes we commit unknowingly when we deal with children of various age groups.

Consider a common scenario. Rohan is a bright, happy child bubbling with energy and studying in fifth standard. He is a bit hyperactive, has a low attention span and therefore, lacks sustained attention to finish various tasks and school homework. Parents attend the 'Parents Teacher Meeting' and the class teacher informs them that Rohan is a bright child but has poor concentration, does not finish his classwork on time, is mostly distracted and his writing is also not legible. He can do better with constant guidance and effort.

All this is told in Rohan's presence. The parents feel dejected and come back home feeling gloomy. Relatives and friends come to meet and gradually the conversation shifts to children and their performance in school. Parents discuss openly in front of the child and repeat the words said by the class teacher.

Many times, during the day, the child keeps hearing such remarks, "Rohan, concentrate on your schoolwork. Your concentration is poor, you are distracted and you are not able to finish your classwork and homework. Your memory is not good and you are unable to remember and recall your lessons. Your handwriting is bad, you better improve it."

The child keeps hearing these remarks from parents and family members who want good for the child and are under the impression that it is their parental duty to keep pointing out the child's shortcomings so that he improves and overcomes them. Little do they realize that unknowingly they are doing so much harm to the child. As we repeat negative statements to the child his subconscious mind accepts each word and starts acting on it. **The subconscious mind is like a child. It has no discriminatory powers. It fails to reject anything. It accepts whatever is given to it literally and completely.**

Gradually, because of this fact, Rohan's concentration deteriorates further. There is no improvement in his writing skills. Schoolwork and homework remain unfinished. Parents wonder what is wrong with their child, completely oblivious that their constant negative remarks are mostly responsible for the condition of the child.

So, what needs to be done?

In this whole scenario, parents can play a significant role by making the required efforts for improvement in the concerned areas, and most important by programming the child's mind with positive and encouraging remarks.

Even if it is not true, we need to tell the child, "Your concentration is excellent. You can focus your concentration at will. Total concentration is yours when you want it. You are a fast learner. Your memory is sharp and you remember what you learn and recall it when the time comes. Your mind is focused towards achieving your goals. Your handwriting is legible and keeps improving with practice. You look forward to challenges and you know you are a winner who achieves his goals."

So, what happens?

The subconscious mind is constantly listening to these positive affirmations, it accepts them literally and starts acting on them. Gradually you watch the positive changes in the child and miracles happen. (The power of the subconscious mind will be discussed further in this book.)

It is like fake it, till you make it!

If you give more attention to negative behaviour, it will grow. If you give more attention to the positive aspects of behaviour, they will grow.

It is that simple.

THE REMOTE IS IN YOUR HANDS

Choose to be happy, the remote is in your hands.

"I trusted my friends and they betrayed me. I feel so cheated."

"The situation at my home is very disturbing. I feel so unhappy, but it is not in my control."

In dealing with clients, we come across many similar scenarios. So many times, we have no control over other people's attitudes or behaviour, nevertheless, it starts affecting us negatively and we feel stressed and disturbed. We can do our best to bring the required changes in the person or the situation. But if that is not possible, then we can choose to keep the remote of our happiness with ourselves and not be affected by the situation and be happy.

Happiness is a concept from within. Often, we give the Remote of our Happiness to someone or some situation.

Get it back!!

Tell Yourself, I Choose to be Happy!!!

Today I make a conscious decision to choose happiness.

Happiness is a choice and we all have the power to exercise this choice. I often use this concept with my clients. It helps them restructure their thoughts. It gives amazing results by changing the way they think.

"There is no Key to Happiness, the Door is always Open."

- Mother Teresa

LEVEL

We are all at a certain level. And that level is not related to our age or qualifications. A person could be in their sixties but the level could be low. A person could be in their twenties but the level could be high. The level includes our attitudes, our mindset and behaviour in general. This is the only thing which will go with us. Nothing else we can take when we leave this earth. There has been a lot of research on this topic.

Dr. Brian Weiss's work is significant in this area. We take birth and we elevate our level with each birth. We are here to learn our lessons. It is the journey of the soul. We need to learn lessons of joy, happiness, kindness, understanding, compassion, forgiveness etc. and unlearn the lessons of violence, hatred, anger, jealousy, and other negative qualities. Obstacles in our lives accelerate our spiritual growth and give us opportunities to learn our lessons. No soul is sent to earth which does not require learning. When all learning is complete, then we are given a choice of whether we want to come back in physical form or not. If we choose to come back, we come back as guides and masters to guide and serve people and take them from darkness to light.

"We are not human beings having a spiritual experience; we are spiritual beings having a human experience."

- Pierre Teilhard de Chardin

The concept of 'Level' gives us a lot of peace in dealing with traumatic relationships. A person will act, speak, and behave according to their level. We get disturbed if someone speaks rudely to us without any relevant reason, or tries to hurt us with sarcastic comments. At such times, we need to remember the word 'Level' and think that he or she is behaving because of his or her level. This thought gives us immediate peace and helps us remain undisturbed. Moreover, we should not suffer because of other people's uncalled-for remarks and attitudes. Like already discussed, we need to keep the remote of our happiness and peace in our hands.

People also get sadistic pleasure in hurting other people because of their level. When we understand this, then we are at peace. At such times, we can thank the Almighty and think that if we had been in such a situation we would not have spoken or behaved in this manner. It is very difficult to change a person's level if they do not want to change. We do not know how many lifetimes they will take to elevate their level. This thought allows us to keep the Remote of our Happiness in our hands. We are what we are, and what we choose to be. We do not become what others tell us or label us with. The whole power lies within.

WHY WE CAN CHANGE?

I am often asked by my clients, "How can I change myself at this age? I have always been like this." The simplest answer to this question is:

As long as we are alive, we can change our thoughts and behaviour.

We are dynamic organizations, open to change. Anything solid and fixed is as good as dead. But is it so easy to change? The answer is 'No.' It is not so easy to change, because the conscious mind is resistant to change. Whether happy or unhappy, we make our comfort zones and start living in them, since outside the comfort zone, the unknown exists, and unknowns represent anxiety to the conscious mind. Comfort zones are good to rest in, but if we start living in our comfort zone, we stagnate and there is no growth.

Psychological flexibility is the essence of normality.

THE SOLUTION FOCUSED APPROACH

In any situation, we have two options - Go on focusing on the problem, magnify it and feel defeated by it, or focus on the solution and find ways to deal with the problem. **When we are stressed, we become a part of the problem. Successful people focus on solutions and be a part of it.** We need to adjust and adapt to the situation. This is an important life skill. Clients often continue focusing on problems. They can be counselled to accept the problem, move forward and focus more on solutions instead.

For example, when the world was battling COVID-19, people who followed the necessary rules and precautions were a part of the solution. Those who chose to ignore important safety protocols posed a threat to society and proved to be a part of the problem. Be in the solution mode, not the problem mode.

USE THE RIGHT ORGAN

"Oh! My room is so messy and disorganized. I don't feel like working in such a room. What to do?"

"Today again I missed out on my exercise. I'm feeling so guilty and lethargic. I wish I could have done my exercise."

"So many notes to write, I have so much incomplete written work. What will I do? How will I attend school tomorrow, the teacher will again scold me."

These are common statements and no less than wishful thinking. We may have indulged in such thoughts, or seen others facing such issues, leading to the person mostly experiencing stress. The more we keep worrying and ruminating in our minds regarding unfinished work, the more stressed we feel.

So, use the right organ!

With your mind the room is not going to be cleaned, you will need to pick up a broom and clean it. With your mind the exercise will not be done, you will need to get on a treadmill and do it. Similarly, with your mind, the notes will not be written, you will need to pick up a pen and start writing in your notebook. Get up and do it with the right organ!

I use this concept with my clients when required, and it works wonders.

LIFE IS LIKE A CUP OF TEA

We fix ourselves a cup of tea. As we start sipping on it, we drift away into thinking of the past or the future, till we snap out and realise that the tea in the cup is over. We often find ourselves wondering, "Did I have my tea?" In contrast, if we pick up the cup and take in the aroma, savour the taste and wrap our hands around the cup to soak in the warmth of the tea, the whole experience becomes wonderful and mindful and it's only then that we say, "Ah! I had an amazing cup of tea."

Life is like this, a cup of tea. It will just pass thinking about the past or the future. The human mind tends to live in the past or the future. We live with the load of the past or future on our shoulders. Past is history or like a cancelled cheque. It will never come back. Tomorrow is a mystery or a promissory note. Tomorrow never comes. When it comes, it becomes today. Today is called the present. It is a gift from The Universe. It is ready cash that we can spend. Most people live in the past or the future. We should train our minds to live in the present and the now.

Mindfulness is paying attention on purpose, in the present moment and without judgment. Through mindfulness, you discover how to live in the present moment in an enjoyable way rather than worrying about the past or future. Mindfulness also helps us to respond, not react. A reaction is automatic and gives you no choice, a response is a deliberate and considered action. Mindfulness encourages us to respond to our experiences rather than react to thoughts.

"Between stimulus and response, there is a space. In that space is our power to choose our response. In our response lies our growth and freedom."

- Victor Frankl

Many a battle in relationships, at home, in the workplace or elsewhere could be averted if we use this space and respond, instead of mindlessly reacting and using negative communication patterns.

Your tongue is like a loaded gun which you carry everywhere.

AVOID ORGAN LANGUAGE

So many times, we come across people saying such sentences.

"Oh, he is a pain in the neck."

"Every time I see him, I get a headache."

"Ye dekho sar ka dard chala aa raha hai."

"He's my backbone. I don't know what I will do if he leaves."

"He's a pain in the ass."

This is organ language.

Due to some past negative experiences, or positive experiences with the concerned person, we often indulge in such remarks casually, little knowing such statements when repeated often, can have a great negative impact on our health. Several case studies confirm that using organ language can have detrimental effects on the body of the person using it.

In one such case, a man was very irritated with a colleague due to certain experiences with him. Every time he had to interact with him at work, the thought supreme in his mind was that 'he's a pain in the ass' and he would voice it loudly too. After some time, this man suffered from piles.

Another case study reveals a person thinking and calling another person, 'a pain in the neck.' This continuous remark ultimately resulted in cervical spondylolysis in the person who used this organ language.

A lady was very dependent on her household help. She had a constant fear that if he left, what would she do? She often told her friends "He is my backbone. What will I do if he leaves?" Time passed, and it so happened that he had to leave and shift to another city. Subsequently, this lady developed severe pain in her back and had to be operated on for a slipped disc.

So casually we use such language for another person. "He is a *sar ka dard*, whenever I see him, I get a headache." Little knowing how much harm we are doing to ourselves. That person to whom the remark is directed is not affected at all. We are only harming ourselves by using such organ language.

Avoid organ language. Your health is in your hands.

THE SERENITY PRAYER

*God, grant me the serenity to accept the things I
cannot change,
The courage to change the things I can,
And the wisdom to know the difference.*

This powerful prayer is a complete therapy and works wonders in changing the mindsets and attitudes of people. I use it extensively with my clients explaining it in detail and how to use it themselves to realize what they are holding on to, and what they need to change in their thought patterns and life.

Many times, in life, we keep fighting the things we just cannot change like the colour of our skin, the relations we are born with, some systems in the organization we are working with, other people's attitudes or what comes out from their mouth and so on. Thinking like this we bring stress in our lives and become helpless and unproductive. If we can change something, then ask for the courage to change that thing or aspect of your life. Be bold and courageous to change it if it can be changed, and if change is possible. If change is not possible, we need to accept it. Acceptance creates peace in our mind.

The last line of the prayer is the most important. It says 'Grant me the wisdom to know the difference, between what I can change and what I cannot change.' We usually miss out on this point and hopelessly and helplessly expect changes in the things that we cannot change. This may lead to frustration, disappointment, and anger. We can choose to make our life a wonderful experience or a terrible disaster. The choice is ours.

You are the architect of your life and you draw the blueprints of its design.

Chapter 4

THOUGHT YOGA

The solution to managing thoughts

Thought Yoga helps you to manage and master your thoughts. We all experience numerous thoughts in 24 hours. Research shows that we give selective attention to approximately 60,000 thoughts per day. That means approximately one thought every second. Around 90% of these thoughts are repeated thoughts. What type of thoughts do we think 90% of the time? Where is our persistence? This is what defines us.

We are what we think 90% of the time.

Thought Yoga involves observing your thoughts and realising how they are affecting your emotions and behaviour. We need to be aware and check our thoughts to discover how these are affecting our reality. Whenever we can we should consciously change our thoughts to alter the outcome. It may be a difficult task to continuously scan your thoughts, but with practice, it becomes more and more natural. Be aware of your thoughts, words, feelings and actions.

Out of 60,000 thoughts we have per day, 80-90% of the thoughts are generally negative. Thoughts have a major influence on our lives. They shape our personality and are responsible for our mental health. It is as if a tape of thoughts is playing in our minds. If it is more of negative thoughts then we are disturbed most of the time. Now we have two options. Firstly, we can choose to stop the tape. But this is seemingly too difficult. We cannot be thoughtless for long periods.

We have another option. We can choose to change the recording of the tape. So how to do that?

There are three steps to manage negative or disturbing thoughts. Let us discuss them.

THREE STEPS TO MANAGE NEGATIVE THOUGHTS

Step 1: Suppression

We need to understand that thoughts are powerless. They have no power of their own. They are like smoke. They come and go and may have no effect on our minds. If we choose to give energy to a particular negative thought, entertain it or give power to it, it will stay back and disturb us.

Suppose someone is at your door and they have come to deliver a message and leave. You invite them to your house for a cup of tea. Now they come in and sit there for maybe half an hour or more since you encouraged them to enter your house. In the same way, negative thoughts will enter and be there in your mind if you entertain or encourage them. The choice is yours, to entertain them or let them go.

We need to suppress or let go of disturbing thoughts with sheer willpower, which we all have to a certain extent. Practice the art of watching your mind all the time and do not entertain or encourage negative thoughts. Try to hold the negative thoughts back by exercising your willpower.

Step 2: Substitution

While holding it back, start replacing the negative thought with a positive thought. Many times, we want to think positively but are unable to do so. At such times we can substitute the negative thought with a positive activity like talking to a friend, reading a book, listening to music, engaging ourselves in a hobby and so on. The idea is to distract ourselves from negative thoughts to positive thoughts or a positive activity.

Step 3: Sublimation

As we continue doing the above two steps, the negative becomes sublimated and fades away. We discover that negative thoughts are slowly evaporating away and are being replaced by more positive thoughts. Gradually we find that our mind is now dominated by more positive thoughts. The ratio has changed. 80-90% positive thoughts and 10-20% disturbing thoughts will still be there, which is okay. We all have our phases of negativity. The power lies in resilience, bouncing back to our original positive and happy self, as soon as possible.

Thoughts are like birds flying in the sky, they come and go, but do not leave any impression on the sky. In the same way, our thoughts come and go, they will not affect our minds if we choose so. Thoughts are our creation; since we create them, we also have the power to choose what we create.

I think_____________ therefore, I am_______________.

This powerful sentence was given by the French philosopher **René Descartes.** This is a fill-in-the-blank sentence. According to this statement, whatever you put in the first blank will come out in the second blank. If you put negative in the first blank, negative will come out in the second blank. If you put positive in the first blank, positive will come out in the second blank. For example:

I think I am unhappy **therefore I am** unhappy.

I think I am positive **therefore; I am** positive.

It is on the concept of **Garbage In, Garbage Out**. The thoughts you put in your mind will eventually come out in your feelings and behaviour. Manage the garbage in your mind or the garbage in your life will become unmanageable. ***You mainly feel the way you think and believe***. We have absolute freedom to think and feel the way we want to.

THOUGHTS

FEELINGS

ACTIONS

You mainly feel the way you think.
Thoughts are translated into behaviour.

POSITIVE THINKING IS A SKILL

Positive thinking implies keeping one's mind free from sadness, dejection, anger, worry, hate, tension and other negative thoughts, resulting from situations and events that are only temporary in nature.

Consider this...

If you're at a party, that too shall pass.
If you're at the movies, that too shall pass.
If you're in school, that too shall pass.
If you are facing a tough time, that too shall pass.

We keep on searching for permanent solutions in a temporary life. Be conscious of and accept this most important reality of life: ***This too shall pass.***

A mind that entertains thoughts of joy and goodwill, that is ready to forgive and forget and promote peace and love is positive. Love is an energy of incredible power and strength. We are all made up of this energy. **Love is the only truth, permanent and eternal. The ability to love and forgive are the tools we have been given to live in this not-so-perfect world.**

YOUR BODY RESPONDS TO STRESS

Persistent mental stress may lead to negative emotions, such as fear, anger, jealousy, chronic anxiety, and depression. It is one of the leading causes of illness and death in the world. Stress causes a complex system of hormones and other chemicals to be released into the body. When stress persists, many organs in the body are exposed to harmful consequences.

Stress causes changes in heart rate, blood pressure and blood sugar levels. Stress also depresses the natural functioning of our immune system, impairing our ability to fight infections and chronic illnesses.

Stress weakens our physical immunity as well as emotional immunity. When we are under stress our mind is dominated by negative or disturbing thoughts.

Decisions made in times of stress often prove to be wrong. We should not trust our thoughts at such a time since they are not reliable at that time and may lead to wrong actions or decisions. **Never make irreversible decisions based on reversible emotions.** Some emotional components of physical conditions are:

- **Anger and stress** – hide in our liver and stomach, affect digestion, and create acidity.
- **Responsibility** – sits heavy on our shoulders, we feel heavy and there is pain.
- **Stubbornness** – may cause neck problems.
- **Past hurt and resentment** - may cause constipation.
- **The feeling of being controlled** – may cause migraine headaches.
- **Financial insecurity** – may cause discomfort in the lower back.

"Anger is only one letter short of Danger."

– Eleanor Roosevelt

Similar situations may have different reactions in different people. Some students take too much stress during exams and are unable to cope with the pressure, leading to anxiety, distress and low performance in their exams. At the same time, other students may not exhibit significant symptoms of stress since they can cope effectively with the pressure faced during exams. Effective coping skills play a major role in managing stressful situations.

Stress is a byproduct of inadequate coping.

PATTERNS OF NEGATIVE THINKING

People often get stuck in repeated patterns of negative thoughts. They typically exhibit one or many of these thought patterns:

- **Critical about themselves** – Such people tend to attribute all their success to outside events and mostly indulge in self-criticism leading to low self-esteem and self-created miseries.

- **Worrying** – Undue worrying about present or future events which are not in one's control.

- **Control thinking** – Wanting to take full control of people and events which becomes impossible and subsequently leads to stress.

- **Obsessive thinking** – Excessive and unreasonable thoughts regarding something leading to compulsive behaviours and preoccupation with an idea or feeling.

Negative thinkers carry their misery, their illness, and their hell within themselves. Avoid being a negative thinking expert.

THOUGHTS HAVE POWER

Thought power is the greatest power we are blessed with. As you think, so shall you become. One can evolve to unimaginable heights by directing the mental processes towards that which is positive.

People typically experience 7 types of thoughts:

- **Toxic Thoughts** - They release harmful chemicals and create toxins affecting our behaviour, energy, and physical body. E.g.: Thoughts of anger, revenge, jealousy, hatred, rejection, fear etc.

- **Negative Thoughts** - Thinking negatively about self and others. E.g., thoughts of failure, loss, illness, anxiety, doubt, control, irritation etc. These may gradually become toxic.

- **Waste Thoughts** - Unnecessary, time wasters, energy leaks.

- **Necessary Thoughts** - Related to what we need to do each day.

- **Right Thoughts** - Whatever the situation, see it as it is without any magnification.

- **Positive Thoughts** - Thoughts of joy, harmony, peace, and love. Positive thinking is a skill that we need to develop.

- **Elevated Thoughts** - Thoughts of higher knowledge and spiritual thoughts, elevate our level.

We think thoughts are situation dependent and getting angry or irritated is natural for us. That's not the case. Peace is natural to us. We are all born as peaceful souls.

Be a Positive Thinking Expert! Positive thinkers carry their happiness, their health, and their heaven within themselves.

Heaven and Hell are not geographical. If you go in search of them, you will never find them anywhere. They are within you. They are psychological. The mind is heaven. The mind is hell. If you are miserable most of the time you are in hell. If you are blissful most of the time you are in heaven. The mind can become either. The choice is yours.

The mind can live in both heaven and hell.

CHANGE YOUR SELF-TALK. CHANGE YOUR REALITY.

Mind is a supercomputer which runs on the program of our self-talk. Your self-talk becomes your reality. What others say about you is not in your control. However, what we say and think about ourselves is totally in our control. What you say to yourself defines who you are. Watch your thoughts! Make conscious efforts to think, believe and say positive things to yourself and also about yourself and then see the miracle! Positive self-talk is a great way of programming the Subconscious Mind.

Some common thoughts which give rise to limiting beliefs:

- 'It can't be done.'
- 'It cannot happen.'
- 'No one could do it.'
- 'I am not worth it.'
- 'It is too difficult.'

Change your self-talk. Change your reality.

- 'Why can't it be done?'
- 'Why can it not happen?'
- 'So, what if no one could do it, I could be the first one!'
- 'How can I make myself worth it?'
- 'How can I master it?'

Expand your boundaries with positive thoughts, and open yourself to higher possibilities.

As we contemplate and study thoughts, we realize what a terrific force they are and what unlimited powers they have. If you glance around, you will find yourself looking at many things. This is your visual perception. In reality, what you are actually looking at is thoughts or ideas which have come into materialization through the creative work of the human mind. It was a thought first that created those things. In the next chapter, let us discuss the source of all thoughts – **The Mind!**

Chapter 5

THE MIND

The mind has an immense direct influence on our nervous system and body. Indirectly mind influences all things around us. Everything good or bad which is man-made on this planet has come twice. First in the mental plane and then it was translated into the physical plane.

For example, we can think of any simple thing or any complicated thing like pen, paper, pencil, computers, mobile phones, social media, artificial intelligence, etc. All these first came into someone's mind and then they came into reality. Someone visualized those things in the mental plane and then these things became reality in the physical plane. This is a fact of life. All inventions, simple and complex, have come up in this way.

Mind, Body, and Behaviour are intimately linked. Everything first enters the mind in the form of a thought and then it is accepted by the body and as a result, it reflects in our behaviour. If we want some changes at the behaviour level, we must work first at the mind level. Our bodies are intimately linked to our minds. So, our moods and emotions are easily translated into physical symptoms, leading to psychosomatic disorders.

Psychosomatic disorders are disorders in which the mind plays a major role in precipitating and maintaining the disorder. Let's understand this with a simple example. Suppose we keep our whole house very clean and tidy, but in one room we dump all the garbage. After some time, a stench will start emitting from that room. Likewise, when stress and anxiety are stored for long periods in the mind, they find an outlet in the form of physical symptoms like headache, acidity, stomach ache, skin problems etc. This is the reason why most doctors, besides prescribing medicines, encourage us to relax and avoid stress.

The mind has the power to create illness and also to heal it. The mind overvalues things it does not have and undervalues things it does have, leading to dissatisfaction and distress. Our thoughts play a major role in keeping a healthy mind and body. Mind power is a vast and powerful inner dimension, and we can learn to use it constructively.

Mind is the ultimate human freedom given to us.

THREE STATES OF THE MIND

The mind has the tendency and the capability to be in varying states, positive or negative. The states of the mind can vary according to people and situations. For better understanding, we can visualise the mind as a mental cone which acquires different positions or states depending on our mindset and the environment we are in. Broadly we can discuss three states of mind in which people seem to live.

<u>**Restless Equilibrium**</u>

- In this state, the mind is constantly restless.
- Such people want everything according to their desires.
- They mostly remain disturbed and agitated *like a cone that rests on its apex and is never stationary.*

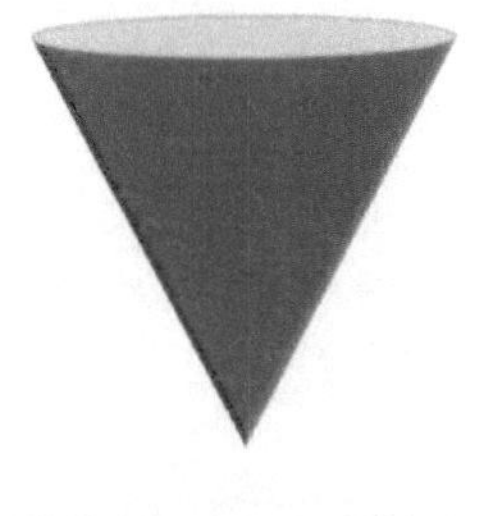

RESTLESS EQUILIBRIUM

<u>**Imperfect Equilibrium**</u>

- Most people fall in this category.
- Mind is balanced most of the time, but it just needs a small stimulus to get affected and once it gets agitated, it lingers.
- Mind is *like a cone which rests on its side.* It is at rest, but if tapped, it oscillates and can go on oscillating for a long time.
- This type of mental agitation is disturbing and causes fatigue.
- Mind can be trained not to be affected. You cannot prevent stimuli in the external world, you can only

prevent your reactions. The stimulus lasts only for a few moments but lingers in your mind for a long time. So, a large part of your energy is wasted in this lingering agitation. Remember, it is not possible to carpet the whole earth, all we can do is wear shoes. Picture your intellect as a cone. Every time the cone oscillates, bring it back to a stationary position.

IMPERFECT EQUILIBRIUM

Suppose you are feeling good and positive at your workplace and doing your work calmly. At that time, your mental cone is at rest and in equilibrium. Suddenly, a colleague passes an uncalled-for negative comment on you. This goes on and on in your mind and your peace gets disturbed, your mental cone starts oscillating and you are no longer at peace. This mental agitation can go on for a long time. You go home after work, but still, the comment lingers in your mind and you keep feeling upset. If this prolongs, your efficiency comes down and you may end up feeling frustrated and sad. In such situations, we can train our mind not to be affected. We can remember that our mind is like a cone and bring our mental cone to a stationary position. This can be done by using counselling concepts like 'level' and 'remote' discussed earlier in this book.

Perfect Equilibrium

- This state of mind is rare and the person having it is free from restlessness.
- Whether placed in the best or worst environment, such people remain calm and collected.
- This does not mean they are without feelings or emotions. They have heightened awareness. They can be poised irrespective of their environment.
- In this state, the mind is ***like a cone which rests on its base and is always stationary.***

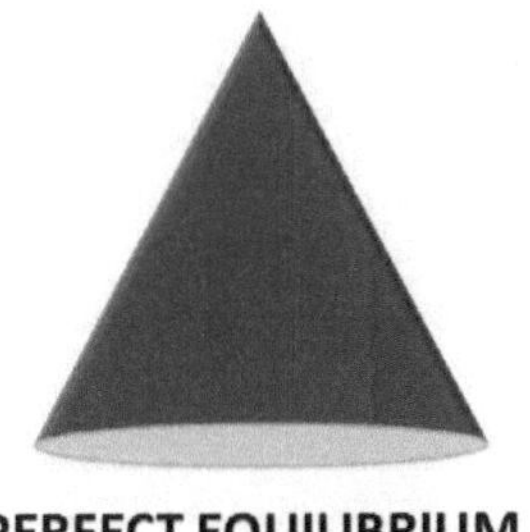

PERFECT EQUILIBRIUM

A Mind without agitation is meditation.

THE STRUCTURE OF MIND

When we talk of the mind, people often confuse it with the human brain. The brain is an organ which we can see, touch, and even operate. But the mind is something abstract, cannot be seen, cannot be touched. Still, a lot of work has been done on the mind. Various researchers have made assumptions about its structure and defined it in their own way. Sigmund Freud, the famous Austrian psychoanalyst, has proposed the Topographical Structure of the Mind.

THE MIND

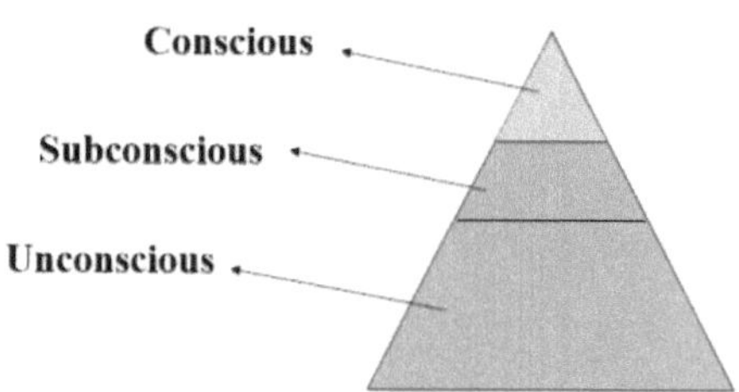

Topographical Structure of the Mind

The human mind, just like an iceberg, consists of two parts:

The conscious mind

The conscious mind is the tip of the iceberg. It is 10-12% of the total mind. It consists of all those mental elements that are in one's awareness at any given moment. It represents our consciousness. Consciousness denotes a state of awareness of one's own self and one's environment which helps us with daily decision-making processes. Thinking, reasoning, analysis, and logical operations are carried out in this part of the mind. It assists us in new or unknown situations where we must apply rational thinking. This part of the mind can also be understood as the critical mind.

The Unconscious Mind

The unconscious mind has two different levels: The subconscious and the unconscious proper.

The Subconscious Mind

The subconscious mind consists of all those mental elements that are not conscious but can become readily available to consciousness with little effort. What a person perceives remains in consciousness for a temporary period and when our attention shifts to something else, it quickly goes into the subconscious, but with little effort, we can recall that information. Thus, the subconscious mind is also called 'available memory'. It stores information for later retrieval. Let us suppose we were involved in an incident a few days ago. If we want to recall it now, we can easily do so, the memory of that experience is not lost. We can easily regain it. The subconscious is the seat of all stored memories. Another quality of the subconscious mind is that it has no logical or rational thinking. It is like a child and accepts everything literally.

The Unconscious Mind

The unconscious mind is the most important and the largest part of the mind. It exists below the surface of awareness and determines behaviour to a large extent. It stores all experiences, memories, conflicts, and repressed materials. The unconscious processes play a significant role in shaping our behaviour. All neurotic symptoms and behaviour are rooted in the unconscious processes and may interfere with healthy functioning.

The unconscious ideas enter the consciousness in a disguised or distorted form, for example, through dreams. Dreams are symbolic representations of unconscious needs, wishes and conflicts. Dreams have manifest content and latent content. What we see in dreams is the *manifest content*. Most dreams, especially recurrent ones have a hidden meaning, also called *latent content*. A censoring process works which converts the actual images into innocent-appearing images so that we do not feel anxious after waking up from the dream. Dreams are said to be the royal road to the unconscious.

A state of greater health is achieved whenever areas of life dominated by unconscious forces are shrunk so that a larger area of life is dominated by conscious or subconscious forces.

THE POWER OF THE SUBCONSCIOUS MIND

The subconscious mind is the instinctive, impulsive, and intuitive part of the mind. The conscious mind sleeps when we are in the sleep state. The subconscious mind never sleeps. It is always awake and controls our actions during sleep. Likewise, it is awake and in control while in the hypnotic state.

The subconscious is like the automobile, while the conscious mind is like the driver. Of the two, the subconscious is more powerful. The power is in the automobile, but the control is with the driver.

The conscious mind is the thinker, the decision maker, and gives instructions to the subconscious mind to obey. The conscious becomes the master, the subconscious the servant. The subconscious can work for us or against us. It does not have any logic or rational thinking. It is like a garden; it does not care what we plant. It is neutral, it has no preferences. If we plant good seeds, we get a good garden, otherwise, we have a wild growth of weeds. Our subconscious mind does not discriminate. Whatever we choose to put into our mind, our subconscious will accept and our behaviour will reflect accordingly. We can access the subconscious mind, eliminate negativity, do away with our limiting beliefs, replace them with more empowering beliefs and reprogram the mind in a positive way to bring lasting changes in ourselves.

PROGRAMMING THE SUBCONSCIOUS MIND

The subconscious mind is the controller of our thoughts, feelings, and behaviour. It also controls all the biological processes going on in our body. The subconscious is a big storehouse of a large number of programs or frames of reference. These programs are created by all the experiences, information, and imaginations that we had since our birth till now. It is like a library with information fed into it every day. Any event or situation in our life is interpreted in the mind based on the relevant program existing in our subconscious. It is the interpretation of the event or situation (and not the situation itself) that gives rise to our thoughts, feelings, behaviour and even our biological processes. It is our internal map and may not be the reality.

Thus, the conscious mind is guided by a particular frame of reference in the subconscious mind for every given situation and we think, feel, and hence behave accordingly. At any juncture of life, if we feel our thinking, feeling, or behaviour is not conducive to our growth, we can bring lasting changes in ourselves by re-programming the subconscious mind.

Our subconscious mind is a treasure house of riches and whatever we desire can be drawn forth from it.

Since the conscious mind is resistant to change, we need to put it into a passive state. Once the conscious mind is passive, one enters into a state of inner absorption, concentration and focussed attention in which suggestions are easily accepted.

A fast and sure way to access the subconscious mind, eliminate negativity and positively reprogram the mind is through hypnosis. Hypnosis and hypnotherapy are powerful tools that can be used to ensure success, growth, and a fulfilling life.

"The mind is like a parachute; it only works when it is open."

- Thomas Robert Dewar

Chapter 6

HYPNOSIS

AND HYPNOTHERAPY

Keep looking at my pendulum without blinking your eyes. Focus on your breathing. Take a few long deep breaths and begin to relax. Let the muscles in all parts of your body be loose and light, let go of all tightness and tension in these muscles.... and relax. With every breath, you are getting more and more relaxed and you are entering into a deeper and deeper state of total, complete, perfect relaxation...

And now as the pendulum touches the spot on your forehead between your eyes, Your eyes will CLOSE!

Now, Sleep... Sleep... Sleep!!

Total...complete...perfect...relaxation.

Have you ever come across or witnessed such a session or even read about it? Yes, this is Pendulum Hypnosis! Even reading about Hypnosis arouses a lot of questions and doubts in our minds. Hypnosis has always been shrouded with mystery and magic; therefore, people have been away from its numerous benefits.

Very early in my career as a Clinical Psychologist, I was drawn to Hypnosis and Hypnotherapy. Even the mention of the word 'hypnosis' in any magazine or newspaper, would catch my attention. I was first exposed to a session of hypnosis in Agra, and I was fascinated! While pursuing my course in clinical psychology, I somehow instinctively knew that I wanted to excel in multiple therapies to alleviate suffering and bring lasting changes in my clients. I learned various therapies from learned teachers and mentors and eventually mastered Hypnotherapy. I urge budding psychologists to do the same. Learning various types of psychotherapies equips one with the necessary tools for successful healing. An eclectic approach involving diverse therapies as per the specific needs of each client is always desirable.

I chose hypnotherapy as my research topic while pursuing a Doctor of Philosophy, Ph.D. in Psychology. My topic of research was, "Role of Hypnotherapy in the Management of Generalized Anxiety Disorder Patients."

It is quite unfortunate that due to various myths and misconceptions surrounding hypnosis, people have been wary of it. For many years, they were unaware of its potential as an effective mode of treatment for many ailments and mental conditions. However, with the current level of awareness surrounding us, it is encouraging to see changing perceptions regarding hypnosis. Hypnotherapy has the power to bring transformational changes in clients and is very effective in solving deep-rooted issues faced by them.

It is extremely important to understand that hypnosis or hypnotherapy cannot be practised merely by reading about it in a book or on the internet. One must get formal practical training in the subject by a trained and competent authorized teacher of hypnosis. Unskilled hypnotherapy can do more harm than good.

HYPNOSIS: AN ALTERED STATE OF CONSCIOUSNESS

Hypnosis has a long history dating back to the 17th century. The first recognizable practitioner of hypnosis was France Anton Mesmer, an Austrian physician who used the power of suggestion to cure illnesses. His technique was called 'Mesmerism.' The term Hypnosis came from a Scottish physician James Braid (1843) who used the Greek word for sleep to create the term. 'Hypnos' means 'sleep' in Greek. It soon replaced the word 'mesmerism.'

Hypnosis is a complex mental phenomenon that has been defined as a state of heightened focal concentration and receptivity to the suggestions of another person. It has also been called an 'altered state of consciousness' (Tart, 1975). It is a dissociated state and an induced state of relaxation in which the person is open to suggestions.

We often refer to the person undergoing hypnosis as 'the subject.' In hypnosis, the brain waves are operating at the 'alpha' level, which is at a frequency of 7-14 Hz. Alpha waves are conducive to hypnosis and meditation, heightened creativity and physical relaxation. This is one of four primary brain wave patterns (the other three being beta, theta and delta) and is measurable on the electroencephalograph (EEG). Alpha state denotes a mentally alert but physically relaxed state. This contrasts strongly with the waves emitted when the subject is asleep, in which all the waves are completely relaxed representing no conscious mental alertness. Sleep thus, is a very different state to a state of hypnotic trance.

Hypnosis is a fast and direct means of getting to the subconscious mind. During hypnosis, the mind settles down to a restful inner alertness, during which it is least excited and is in a silent state of awareness. The mind is perfectly calm and collected, yet fully awake and fully expanded. Thus, a unique state of rest is achieved. A general sense of well-being prevails. Once the subject is deeply relaxed and focused, they are in a state of hyper-suggestibility and easily influenced by suggestions. The hypnotherapist can then give any positive suggestions for improvement that will have very long and lasting effects on the subject.

Hypnosis can be understood as attentive, receptive focal concentration with diminished peripheral awareness. This intense concentration can be actively initiated and structured to achieve agreed-upon goals. In hypnosis, the subject is comfortably detached from the everyday world, with conscious thinking minimized.

Hypnosis is a form of deep relaxation and only a shift of consciousness where the inner subconscious takes the front seat and is in control, while the conscious relaxes comfortably in the back seat. A state of deep relaxation means that you are relatively free of the usual busy thought traffic that bombards your mind in everyday consciousness. In the absence of all the usual distracting clutter, your mind is able to direct itself inward and achieve a depth of focus not normally accessible in the ordinary waking state.

Hypnosis is a state of dual awareness. Some parts of the mind are in the conscious state and some parts in the altered state, also known as the trance state. In the altered state, we can access the subconscious mind. It accepts healthy and helpful suggestions. Since some part of the mind is conscious, it will always analyze and refrain from doing anything against the person's will and moral values.

Research proves hypnosis and auto-suggestions can have organic physiological effects. Hypnosis works on the body via the mind (Water Field, in his beautiful book, 'Hidden Depths-The Story of Hypnosis').

With appropriate therapeutic design, this variant of imagination can be activated, identified, measured, controlled, and used for specific therapeutic purposes.

Under Hypnosis:

- There is no loss of consciousness.
- The subjects never tell their innermost secrets if they do not want to.
- The subjects never surrender their will.
- The subjects are in contact with reality.

***All Hypnosis, in essence, is Self-hypnosis.**_

Hypnosis is often seen as caused by the hypnotist's special powers or mysterious abilities. The reality is that the hypnotist has no special powers but the skill of inducing hypnotic trance (deep relaxation). The hypnotist offers suggestions that the subject may or may not choose to respond to. Hypnosis works and is effective only when the subject cooperates, surrenders, and chooses to be hypnotized.

Important Differences

Sleep and Hypnotic state

- In sleep, there is no conscious mental alertness. During the sleep state, we do not learn. In a hypnotic state, the subject is aware of what is happening and learning is possible.
- Sleep and communication cannot be done simultaneously. On the other hand, lengthy communication is possible in the hypnotic state.

Hetero-hypnosis and Self-hypnosis

- Hetero-hypnosis is a hypnotic state that is created by another person. It involves a hypnotist or hypnotherapist inducing the hypnotic state in a subject by various induction techniques.
- Self-hypnosis is a hypnotic state that is self-created when a person goes into a hypnotic state by himself/herself using self-hypnosis techniques.

- Listening to an audio and reaching a hypnotic state is not self-hypnosis, rather it is hetero-hypnosis since trance is being induced by someone else's voice.

Suggestions

- One of the best ways of influencing the subconscious mind is through suggestions.
- Every person is suggestible to some degree, extremely so while under a hypnotic trance.
- Being suggestible is a benefit. If you were not suggestible, you would never be able to learn.
- When suggestions are repeated many times, they become more effective. The more an idea is repeated the more likely it is to be accepted by the subconscious mind and acted upon by the subject. For example, advertisements work on repeated suggestions and thus have the power to influence our minds.

HYPNOSIS: MYTHS AND MISCONCEPTIONS

Hypnosis is surrounded by many myths & misconceptions, which has kept many people away from its tremendous benefits. Some common myths are:

- Hypnosis is caused by the hypnotist's special power.
- Hypnotists can control the mind and make people do anything and reveal all their secrets.
- Trance is a state of complete loss of consciousness.

- If the hypnotist leaves the subject in a trance state, the subject will never be able to get out of the trance.
- Only a weak-minded person can be hypnotized.
- A person can be hypnotized against his will.

The Truth

MYTH	THE TRUTH
• There may be use of some magic, *'mantra,'* *'tratak'* or supernatural power in hypnosis.	✓ Every hypnosis is self-hypnosis
• Only people with weak willpower can be hypnotised.	✓ There is no relation between willpower and hypnotic susceptibility. ✓ Some studies have shown a positive relationship.
• A person in hypnosis will lose control of themselves.	✓ During hypnosis, the person in trance always remains in full control if they choose to be.
• A person may reveal secrets during hypnosis.	✓ Secrets are never revealed during hypnosis. ✓ Sometimes encapsulated memories of traumatic life events may surface.

• A person will not remember, upon awakening, whatever transpired during hypnosis.	✓ Amnesia, a partial or total loss of memory of the hypnotic session is one of the several phenomena of hypnosis present only in about 5% of people. ✓ There may be partial amnesia in about 30% of people.
• A person may remain in hypnosis for an indefinite period, if not awakened by the therapist.	✓ If not awakened by the therapist, the person will come out of hypnosis on their own within 5 to 7 minutes. ✓ Generally, the person has good control throughout the hypnotic trance.

WHAT IS HYPNOTHERAPY?

The therapeutic application of hypnosis is known as hypnotherapy. It provides an opportunity for self-mastery by making the subjects aware of their unconscious potential and by increasing their ability to produce desirable changes in their habit patterns, motivations, self-image, and lifestyle in general.

Hypnotherapy is goal-oriented and effective in the treatment of many psychosomatic disorders and other medical problems, especially where stress is one of the causative factors. Hypnotherapy works on cause and effect. Every problem (effect) has a cause and when that cause is eliminated from the subconscious mind, the problem vanishes. Through hypnosis, we access the reason for the problem within the unconscious mind, bring the problem to the surface (conscious mind) and then deal with it. Hypnotherapy debugs your system, deletes the viruses (old unhealthy patterns that are corrupting the system) and replaces them with new, healthy and desirable patterns. Using the power of suggestions, positive changes are made by reprograming the mind under trance.

TRANCE

Trance is best defined as 'Inward focus.' Trance induced during hypnosis is a natural state of the mind that allows it to be connected to both the inside and the outside world at the same time. It is a state of dual awareness. The three states of consciousness are Awake, Sleep and Dream. Hypnosis is the fourth state of consciousness, an altered state and a very powerful one, which can be used to bring lasting changes.

There are naturally occurring trance states as well, which we encounter daily. These may include daydreaming, reading a good book, watching an interesting movie, listening to a story and getting completely absorbed in it, oblivious to the surroundings. In such times, we go into a different state of awareness, which is the naturally occurring state of trance.

Trance may be mild, moderate or intense in depth. Milton Erickson (1950), a pioneer in clinical hypnotic induction, described the process of trance as a 'free period in which individuality can flourish.'

Hypnotherapy has cured or alleviated an enormous range of illnesses and ailments. The below list touches upon some of its uses. The power of hypnotherapy goes much beyond.

SOME USES OF HYPNOTHERAPY

✓ Mental Health and Physical Fitness
✓ Full Alertness and Creative Intelligence
✓ Improved Interpersonal Relations and Job Satisfaction
✓ Reduced Insomnia, Headaches and Pain
✓ Improved Cardiovascular Health & Coping
✓ Managing negative thoughts and limiting beliefs and promoting positive ones
✓ Treating Psychosomatic Problems and Habit disorders
✓ Stress Management
✓ Increased Self Confidence, Will power and Self-esteem
✓ Motivation & Goal Achievement
✓ Improved Memory, Concentration and Learning Ability
✓ Higher Efficiency and Productivity
✓ Overcoming Fears, Phobias and Addictions
✓ Getting rid of Depression and Anxiety
✓ Overcoming specific habits and developing new abilities

- ✓ Improved Quality and Performance in various spheres – personal, professional, study and sports
- ✓ More Energy & Vitality
- ✓ Creating Meditative Awareness
- ✓ Helping you to help others

Present Status

Hypnotherapy has been recognized as a legitimate form of treatment method by the:

- British Medical Council (1955)

- The American Medical Association (1958)

- Medical Councils of countries including Canada, Australia, Sweden and Japan.

- The Ministry of Health & Family Welfare, Government of India (2003). It has stated that Hypnotherapy is a recognized mode of therapy in India.

- The Indian Society for Clinical & Experimental Hypnosis (ISCEH), established in 1972.

Chapter 7

CASE STUDIES

With this background of therapeutic interventions, in the following chapters, I will be sharing some real-life cases where different therapies were used effectively to resolve the client's diverse issues. I hope these revelations are helpful and provide a guideline to readers, professionals, as well as students. All names and places have been changed to maintain confidentiality.

Hypnotherapy, Age Regression and Cord Cutting Technique to Alleviate Blood Phobia

(In a single session)

Reema, a 26-year-old female client visited me with a lot of anxiety at the sight of blood. She was a trained physiotherapist, but due to her condition could not work in any hospital. She had already taken anti-anxiety medicines, but her problem remained unresolved. She was suffering from haemophobia, commonly known as blood phobia.

Haemophobia or blood phobia is the extreme and irrational fear of blood, often caused by trauma or injury in childhood or adolescence. Affected persons, upon viewing blood, display typical reactions like anxiety, nausea, increased blood pressure and heart rate.

Hypnotherapy, Age Regression and Cord Cutting Techniques were used to alleviate blood phobia in the client. Symptoms included anxiety, nausea, and dizziness at the sight of blood due to unknown reasons. The client's fear was marked, persistent and unreasonable, resulting in conscious avoidance of specific situations. She found the symptoms unusual and strange, but could not understand the cause. Psychotherapeutic techniques and pharmacotherapy had failed to relieve her from the discomfort and fear. Hypnosis was used to explore the subconscious or unconscious mind and uncover hidden causes. Initial sessions of the hypnotic intervention included breath watching and Progressive Muscle Relaxation (PMR), to induce trance. Positive pleasant imagery was suggested under trance. Suggestions were given to visualize a very safe and peaceful place, like a beautiful garden. The client was told to see herself in the garden, surrounded by a ball of pure white healing light.

Insight Generation

Age regression brought deep-seated issues of anxiety to the surface and helped the client to recover repressed memories and the resultant trauma. The client could recall that at the age of six, she saw herself playing in the garden of her house. She was all alone and while playing, she hurt herself on her ankle with a sharp stone. She had injured herself and was bleeding profusely. She was in pain and experienced fear on seeing blood. It was traumatic since she was all alone and felt deserted. She recalled crying bitterly and eventually losing consciousness. She had fainted and might have the traumatic memory repressed in her unconscious mind. She could relive the entire trauma vividly.

During the intervention, an additional Cord Cutting process was done to free the client of her fear and alleviate the symptoms of anxiety. On suggestion, she could see the whole scene on a screen and visualize a cord that was attaching her to the screen, a cord that tied her to her past trauma. She could see a thick black cord connecting her to the screen. On further suggestion, she was able to cut the cord which tied her to her past, thus freeing herself.

As a post-hypnotic suggestion, she was told that she would continue to experience this freedom even after the session was over. Suggestions for ego strengthening and enhancing confidence, willpower, and self-esteem were given. After awakening from the hypnotic trance, she recalled the whole scene vividly and cried profusely. I gathered her in my arms, consoled her and helped her release pent-up emotions. The session brought about immediate catharsis and relief from symptoms, resulting in a state of relaxed mind and body.

The Cord Cutting Technique is all about disconnecting from difficult thoughts, emotions, relationships, or negative events from the past. Cutting these negative cords releases fear, resentment, and anger that one may have been holding onto without realizing. It helps to disconnect the negative cord of attachment that exists between the negative event and the individual. Through the cord-cutting technique, the client was able to detach, let go of her past and free herself from fear.

Follow-up Session

The client reported normal responses to the sight of blood in the monthly follow-up sessions. She reported increased energy, self-esteem, and confidence. She had healed the painful memories locked away in her unconscious mind. Thus, she was able to change her reactions to the past and start afresh.

Important to Remember

The Cord Cutting Technique only releases attachments that have turned negative, that drain, cripple and harm us in some way and not positive, loving aspects of relationships. Many times, memories of past events affect our present and our future as well. It is important to let go of the past, free ourselves and live a fulfilling life.

We are mostly suffering our memories; we need to let go and experience emotional freedom from memories.

Systematic Desensitization to Deal with Exam Anxiety

Juhi, a 23-year-old student, was brought to me by her mother. She was suffering from severe depression. There were cut marks on her wrist, from suicidal attempts. She was pursuing Bachelor of Dental Surgery from a private college in Delhi, away from her home town. She was living in the college hostel. In the second semester, she failed three subjects, scoring just two or three marks less than the minimum passing criteria. While taking the case history, she shared that a particular teacher who held some personal grudges against her had purposely given her lower marks in those subjects. Juhi had always been a very bright student and had never experienced failure in her academic career. When the result was declared, she was shocked and was unable to accept it. As time passed, she started keeping quiet and withdrawn and even stopped talking to her family. She lost her appetite and started losing weight.

The symptoms worsened with time. She was diagnosed with severe depression. When Juhi's mother approached me for counselling and therapeutic intervention, she was already on anti-depressants. When I met Juhi, she would hardly talk. With great difficulty and a lot of patience, I could take the case history, coaxing her to share whatever she was going through. I made her feel safe and assured her confidentiality. Slowly, with a lot of gaps in conversation and much resistance, she was able to share her plight. She cried easily. Her mother shared that the college gave three attempts to reappear in the required exam. However, due to her condition, Juhi missed two of them. In one attempt, her family managed to take her to college for the exam but as soon as she entered the college premises, she fainted. She was unable to write the exam.

Now, the main concern was that this was the third attempt and Juhi's last chance to clear the semester. The exam was scheduled to take place two months from the day we met. We started therapeutic intervention and many sessions were conducted. Each time they travelled from another city for the sessions. The focus was mainly on cognitive restructuring and practising relaxation techniques to manage anxiety. In the second month of treatment, Systematic Desensitization as an intervention to deal with her condition was conducted.

Systematic Desensitization, developed by Joseph Wolpe (1958), is a therapeutic technique useful in reducing fears, phobias, and anxiety. The process involves graded exposure to the fearful situation in a prescribed manner. The client is asked to imagine a fearful situation while in a state of deep relaxation. It is based on reciprocal inhibition, which means two mutually opposing responses cannot occur simultaneously. Both anxiety and relaxation are antagonistic to one another and cannot occur together. The relaxation response is first built up and then an anxiety-provoking scene is imagined in this relaxed state. Relaxation, which is the opposing response to anxiety, inhibits it.

Steps in Systematic Desensitization

Relaxation training – The client learns relaxation skills using relaxation procedures with the therapist.

Constructing an anxiety hierarchy – The therapist and client develop a hierarchy of fear-producing stimuli by arranging the items of hierarchy from the least to the most anxiety-provoking. They prepare a graded list of 15-20 scenes in order of increasing anxiety.

In this case study, the following hierarchy was constructed with Juhi's involvement:

1. Announcement of the date of the exam.
2. Getting seats booked for travel to Delhi on the relevant date.
3. Studying for the exam.
4. One week left to leave for Delhi.
5. Packing started for travel to Delhi.
6. Finally, the day has arrived when she must leave for Delhi.
7. She is at the railway station, about to board the train.
8. She is on the train and the journey has started.
9. She reaches Delhi.
10. She enters her college gate.
11. She is in her hostel room.
12. She enters the examination hall.

13. She fills in the required information in the answer sheet, before starting the exam.
14. She reads the question paper.
15. She is relaxed and starts writing her exam.
16. She finishes answering all the questions and hands over the answer sheet to the invigilator.
17. She is relaxed and happy and thinks of a positive outcome.

These items were further elaborated into vivid scenes by the therapist while conducting the desensitization session.

Actual Desensitization

The level of anxiety is assessed on SUDS (Subjective Unit of Distress Scale.) The client is asked to rate the anxiety on a grade of 1 to 10, by thinking about each item of the hierarchy. Desensitization is done systematically by having the client proceed through the list from the least anxiety-provoking scene to the most anxiety-provoking scene, while in a deeply relaxed state. The client practices relaxation with eyes closed, while the therapist describes scenes from the hierarchy.

For desensitization, Juhi was put into a relaxed state using guided imagery. In this relaxed state, the first scene from the hierarchy was presented to her and she was told to vividly imagine the scene. If no anxiety was experienced, then the second scene was presented in a relaxed state. This process continued until all the scenes were presented to her. At any stage, if while visualizing or imagining a scene, she experienced anxiety, she was told to give a signal to me by raising her index finger, while still keeping her eyes closed. The presentation of the scene was immediately stopped, and she was again guided into a relaxed state.

This is called **'ideomotor signalling'**, in which an *idea* is conveyed through a *motor* movement. This technique is often used in hypnotherapy and in conditions where the client is supposed to give a signal of what he or she is feeling without opening the eyes.

In Juhi's case, the whole hierarchy was presented to her till she could visualize all the scenes without any anxiety or with minimal anxiety. The visualization of all the items in the hierarchy took a few sessions. Care was taken to terminate a session in a relaxed state and not let her leave in an anxious state. In the next session, we resumed the desensitization process by presenting the same scene in which she experienced anxiety in the previous session, before moving on to the next item in the hierarchy.

When clients can vividly imagine the scenes in the anxiety hierarchy without discomfort, they experience very little anxiety in real-life situations. They are instructed to see everything in their mind's eye, making the scenes real. Creative visualization works not because you are seeing an image in your mind and it is causing some magic in you. It works because in some way you are shifting the belief system in your mind. Your brain and subconscious mind cannot differentiate between vivid visualization and reality, between an imagined experience and a real experience. It is because of this fact that we start feeling a sour taste in our mouth when we vividly imagine biting into a ripe lemon.

The mental screen is the only place where we can have 100% perfection.

Juhi practised systematic desensitization in the therapeutic sessions with me. Gradually, she felt relaxed, more confident and at ease with the situation. She could finally go to Delhi to take her exam. Today, she is a practising dentist.

Behaviour Modification to Manage Nail-biting with Habit Reversal Training

Rhea, a 25-year-old bright girl visited me one day. She worked as a receptionist in a well-known organization. As part of her job, she was required to meet many people throughout the day. She had the ***nervous habit*** of biting her nails. She had acquired this habit during her childhood and it only grew over time. As she approached her teenage, she tried her best to control this habit but was unsuccessful. She was tempted to bite her nails whenever she felt tense and whenever she watched TV or surfed the net.

As a result of this nervous habit, she had bitten her nails to the extent that now she had nothing left to bite anymore so she started biting the skin surrounding her nails too. Her hands became unpleasant to look at, and she was quite aware of this. She longed to have beautiful nails, so she could wear nail polish in vibrant colours and show them off. She often hid her hands purposely while interacting with people. She felt embarrassed because of how her nails looked, and at the same time helpless, since she was unable to control biting her nails.

Rhea's parents had started looking for a suitable matrimonial match for her. She was looking forward to getting married as well. She finally met someone she liked a lot, and after a few interactions, they decided to get married. Whenever she would meet him, she would be very aware of her disfigured nails and would carefully hide them in one way or the other. They eventually decided to get engaged and their engagement date was fixed for a month later.

Rhea realized that she would now not be able to hide her nails anymore. She would have to show her hand for the exchange of rings during the engagement ceremony. That thought created a lot of anxiety and frustration in her. This disturbed her and she decided firmly that she would now get rid of the habit of biting her nails. It was then that Rhea approached me with her problem.

After taking the case history, a few sessions of relaxation training were administered. Nail-biting is a nervous disorder. The base of nervous disorders is mostly anxiety, for which the client may not be able to give any specific reason and may also not remember the age and time when such a habit developed. After a few relaxation sessions, the client was given **Habit Reversal Training**, which is a Behaviour Modification Technique to manage nervous disorders. The training included the following steps:

Awareness Training

Habits mostly occur unconsciously. The person is usually not aware that he or she is indulging in the habit. Rhea was taught to identify the moment when the nail-biting habit occurred or when it was about to occur. She was trained to become aware of each instance of the habit.

Competing Response Training

A competing response is a behaviour incompatible with the habit behaviour. As a competing response to her nail-biting behaviour, Rhea was taught to grasp a pencil for 1 to 3 minutes or clench her fist for 1 to 3 minutes and hold it by her side. She could also put her hand in her pocket for 1 to 3 minutes as a competing response and let the feeling of biting her nails just pass. She was asked to implement this competing response immediately after becoming aware of each instance of the feeling of biting her nails. In case the habit did occur, she was asked to implement the competing response immediately after each occurrence of the habit. This was practised many times in the therapeutic session. The competing response should always be a behaviour that does not draw attention to the client and goes unnoticed by others.

Social Support

Social support from Rhea's mother was taken for her to continue implementing the competing response behaviour outside the therapy session. Her mother was asked to prompt her to use the competing response whenever she indulged in her habit at home, outside her home, or in other situations.

Motivational Support

Rhea's mother was also asked to praise her for not engaging in nail-biting for extended periods and for using the competing response successfully. A lot of motivation and positive reinforcement in the form of appreciation was given to Rhea. To add to the reinforcement, other things which she liked were arranged by her mother. Rhea was also taught **Self-Management** techniques which involve managing one's own behaviour. Using this, she could monitor her undesirable behaviour and give herself a suitable reward when she was able to control her habit for a significant period.

In the follow-up sessions, Rhea reported that she was able to manage her habit and control nail-biting to a significant extent. Gradually, she could overcome the habit completely and with time, the skin around her nails also healed. She finally looked forward to her engagement ceremony.

A few months later, Rhea met me with sweets, proudly displaying the engagement ring on her beautiful hand. The colour of her nail polish was bright pink.

Behavioural Contract to Manage Strained Relationship

Rahul and Sunita, a young couple, had been married for five years. Initially, they were staying with Rahul's parents. Both were working professionals. After five years, Rahul was transferred to another city. They both shifted to that place and started living on their own. Though they had engaged a house help to do the cooking, there were many other household chores to be done every day. Initially, they distributed the responsibilities but sometimes one or the other partner would fail to fulfil them. This gradually led to a lot of arguments and discord. It got worse with each passing day and finally, both started blaming each other for small issues.

As time passed, the relationship got strained and they were hardly talking to each other. Both were unhappy. However, they wanted things between them to improve. Good sense prevailed and they decided to visit a therapist.

They approached me with their problem. After taking the case history and understanding the issues on which arguments were mostly based, it was suggested that they enter into a behavioural contract in the presence of the therapist. **Behavioural Contracts** are often used by people who want to increase the level of desirable behaviours or decrease the level of undesirable target behaviours.

A target behaviour is a behaviour that a person wants to modify or change. A Behavioural Contract is a written agreement between two parties in which one or both parties agree to engage in a specified level of a target behaviour. They are both displeased with each other's undesirable behaviours or lack of desirable behaviours.

A **Bilateral Contract** or a **Two-party Contract** was made between Rahul and Sunita. This contract is written between two parties, each of whom wants to change a target behaviour. Each party is displeased with some undesirable behaviour of the other party, leading to disturbed relationships. The contract identifies behaviour changes that will be pleasing to both parties.

TWO-PARTY CONTRACT

Date __________ to __________

For the coming week I, Rahul Verma, agree to the following tasks:
1)   I will buy the groceries.
2)   I will load the washing machine.
3)   I will vacuum the carpets.

For the coming week I, Sunita Verma, agree to the following tasks:
1)   I will water the plants.
2)   I will load the dishwasher.
3)   I will do dusting of the house.

Signed: _________________ _________________ _________________
            Rahul Verma   *Sunita Verma*   *Therapist*

The contract made between Rahul & Sunita

This Behavioural Contract worked well with Rahul and Sunita. They were asked to implement the contract for one week and then visit again for follow-up sessions every week.

In the follow-up session, they shared that they were able to implement the contract. Upon successful completion of the contract for a week, reinforcement was added, wherein Rahul and Sunita were asked to reward themselves with one common activity they both liked doing. This was done to break the monotony and ensure compliance of contracts. Rahul and Sunita both loved going to the movies. They shared that after four months, they watched a movie together.

In the subsequent sessions, Rahul and Sunita mutually decided and added more target behaviours that needed to be changed for the smooth functioning of the household. In the weekly sessions, they shared their concerns and relevant solutions were provided. Gradually, things settled down and the relationship improved. Happiness and peace were restored.

Rahul and Sunita realized the importance of shared responsibilities.

Token Economy
to Promote Desirable Behaviour

Rudra, a 7-year-old boy was brought to me by his mother. She was very disturbed due to his undesirable and defiant behaviour at home. He would not listen to her and would trouble her for simple issues. He mostly came home from school with incomplete classwork. He would procrastinate doing his homework most of the time. Rudra's mother felt helpless and had to resort to shouting for him to complete simple tasks, like waking up in the morning, brushing his teeth, having a bath, keeping his things in proper places, and completing his homework.

Nothing seemed to work and the situation was getting worse by the day, leading to a lot of stress and a disturbed environment at home.

Rudra was studying in the fourth grade in a reputed school. After a counselling session with the child, I asked him if he was interested in playing a game, in which he would get many gifts. He immediately said yes. Then I asked him which colour he liked best. He said red.

I included his mother in the session and told the boy that he would be playing this game with his mother. The name of the game was 'Star Game.' Rudra listened intently and with much interest. I explained the game to him and his mother. I told his mother to get a piece of red paper, cut stars out of it and keep them with her.

Next, she was supposed to give Rudra a red star each time he exhibited a desirable behaviour which he had not shown earlier. For example, getting up in the morning when his mother woke him, brushing his teeth, taking a bath, bringing home completed classwork from school and completing his homework.

For every completed activity, Rudra would get one star. He could thus win stars every day for desirable behaviours. Upon collecting a total of ten stars, he could give these stars to his mother and exchange them for a suitable gift that was possible for her to get for him.

This game was to be played every day. Each day, Rudra could win stars and exchange them for desirable gifts. He could even collect many stars and then exchange them for a bigger gift. His mother had the authority to decide which gift he deserved for a certain number of stars won by him.

This is an important Behaviour Modification technique called **Token Economy.** Target behaviours that need to be modified are identified and tokens are delivered immediately after a desirable behaviour. These tokens are later exchanged for some reinforcers at a predetermined exchange rate. Reinforcers may be material, activity or social.

Material reinforcers include some toy or any tangible item desired by the child. Activity reinforcers include an activity the child desires, like an outing or allowing him to watch his favourite TV program. Social reinforcers include encouraging the child with a pat on his back, positive remarks like 'Very Good!' and genuine praise for the child.

In this case, red stars would serve as tokens for Rudra. He was also told about one rule for the star game. The rule was that if he did not indulge in desirable behaviour after being told by his mother many times, he would have to lose one star from the stars he had already won and give it back to his mother. This is called **Response Cost** and is often implemented with a token economy to decrease undesirable behaviours. You must pay a cost for your undesirable response. Rudra agreed to the rules of the game and started playing it with his mother.

Rudra was winning stars every day. In the follow-up sessions, his mother shared that his disruptive and undesirable behaviours had reduced significantly. He had started enjoying the game and had won many gifts too.

This technique works very well with children. It is very effective in modifying behaviour and promoting desirable behaviours. Fading of the token economy should be implemented once desirable behaviours have been learnt and positive changes are in place.

Parents may ask that by implementing this process, they are promoting or teaching the child bribery. It is always desirable to tell them that this behaviour modification technique is a reinforcement technique for modifying behaviour and promoting desirable behaviour. Bribery, on the other hand, is an immoral act for selfish and dishonest interest. There is a difference between the two. Psychoeducation can be given and the difference can be explained to the parent and the child.

Every child is a different kind of flower, and all together, make this world a beautiful garden.

Managing Beer Addiction with Hypnotherapy

Rakesh, a man in his early thirties, approached me with his problem of addiction. He was addicted to beer, especially Budweiser, a variety of beer available in cans and bottles. He would drink 6 to 8 cans every day. Sometimes the number would exceed.

Time was no barrier. He would drink at any time of the day or night. He would often reach home under the influence of the drink, in a dishevelled condition. Rakesh had started facing problems at home due to this addiction. There were constant heated arguments with his father and his wife. His father would often scold him and urge him to leave the habit. Things got worse and one day, Rakesh's wife threatened to leave him if his habit continued.

Rakesh's work suffered too, but he could just not control himself. He enjoyed drinking beer a lot and felt helpless. He would often take a resolve to abstain from it, but soon enough would go back. Rakesh wanted to let go of his habit, so he met me.

His case history revealed that he got into this drinking habit during his college days and it continued, with the quantity increasing as years passed. Over time, he required a greater and greater quantity of beer to experience the same intoxication, indicating tolerance and psychological dependence on the substance.

After the initial counselling sessions, I suggested hypnotherapy to let go of his addiction. He was initially sceptical about the efficacy of the therapy, but since he was motivated to leave the habit, he agreed. The myths and misconceptions surrounding hypnotherapy were explained to him and a consent form was signed. A particular date was mutually decided upon.

On the day of the session, I instructed him to refrain from drinking beer and come for therapy without ingesting any alcohol. He agreed. We proceeded with the hypnotherapy session in the following five phases.

1.   Preparation

This involved having Rakesh sit comfortably in a recliner chair and making him feel at ease.

2.   Induction

This involved breath-watching and Progressive Muscle Relaxation to take Rakesh from normal awareness to a state of trance or enhanced relaxation.

3.   **Deepening**

In the deepening phase, Rakesh was taken from a very relaxed state into a fully hypnotized state. In this state, conscious thinking was minimized.

4.   **Purpose**

In the hypnotic state, Rakesh was given the following suggestions to achieve the goal of therapy:

"As you relax more and more, reflect for a moment on all the successes you have had in the past, the many positive goals that you have already achieved and feel proud of. You feel proud of all the positive aspects of your life, your creativity, your intelligence, and you feel very happy... now because you have been successful in the past...because you have achieved so many positive goals...you will continue to be successful in every area of your life."

"You are now more motivated and more determined than ever before to reject all that is unhealthy and harmful for you...bad habits, tension, stress, and the habit of drinking beer...you now reject this habit of drinking beer. You have all the right reasons to reject any form of alcohol and be a non-drinker. You do it for yourself, for your health and well-being...and that feels fine. You now choose to be a non-drinker...and now see yourself as a non-drinker...you are a non-drinker...and that feels good. You reject the habit of drinking, your mind rejects it, your body rejects it."

"Now, just imagine throwing a bottle of beer out of the window, away from yourself and your life...and you feel great!

You have made up your mind, you have chosen to be a non-drinker and that feels fine. Your body now rejects any harmful thing like beer or any other type of alcohol. Your body wants to become healthy and strong. The smell of beer is now disgusting. The taste of beer is unappealing and horrible. Whenever you hold a can or a bottle of beer in your hand to drink it...you will feel dizzy and very uncomfortable...you will experience nausea and you will feel like vomiting and you will continue to experience these feelings until you discard that can or bottle of beer. After discarding the bottle, you will feel normal...and you will be fine."

"You now choose to be healthy...to be strong...to be clean and fresh. You have made up your mind. You now want a positive life for yourself. You are now a non-drinker. You now make a conscious choice to abstain from drinking beer and you feel just fine. You are a non-drinker. This positive feeling will stay with you throughout this day, and even after this session is over, this feeling will stay with you, and this positive feeling will grow stronger with each passing day..........Relax."

5.   Awakening

In this phase, Rakesh was taken out of the hypnotic state and was brought back to the state of awareness with the conscious mind fully re-engaged.

Post Hypnotic Counselling

After coming out of the trance, Rakesh felt quite relaxed. That time, he felt confident that he could overcome his habit. After some post-hypnotic counselling, he agreed to see me for the next session on a mutually agreed date.

That same day in the evening, I got a call from Rakesh. He seemed quite excited. He told me that since he had not taken beer before the hypnotherapy session, as was agreed upon and promised by him, he thought that he would now have some beer in the evening.

Although he went through the hypnotherapy session, he was not fully convinced that it would work and took it lightly. He purchased a can, and as was his usual practice, opened it to have in his car.

To his utter surprise, as soon as he opened it and wanted to drink it, he started feeling very uneasy. He felt some nausea and felt unwell. The smell of beer was not appealing at all. He tried to drink it but could not bring himself to do so. Rakesh was not able to understand what was happening. Eventually, after struggling for some time, he threw the can into the dustbin. He started feeling better. Rakesh was shocked.

Rakesh visited for seven more sessions and after each session, his resolve to leave his habit grew stronger and stronger. He abstained from drinking beer. His relationship with his wife improved, and the environment at home got better. He was able to focus on his work and started feeling good about himself. He shared that there were weak moments when he felt like drinking, but was not able to do so.

Later, he visited me twice a month for follow-up sessions for three months. At the appropriate time, the therapy was terminated and he was given the assurance that he could contact me anytime.

Hypnotherapy has the power to facilitate deep and lasting inner transformation, safely and effectively.

Managing Religious Beliefs with A Special Session of Hypnotherapy

Rajkumari, a 42-year-old woman approached me for consultation with her husband. She lived about 60 kilometres away in a small district. For the past 15 days, she had been suffering from intense anxiety and constant negative thoughts. She seemed quite depressed.

Her case history revealed that she was a very religious lady. She lived with her husband and two grown-up sons. She worshipped Goddess Durga and had an idol of the Devi at her home. Most of her time went in praying to the Goddess, preparing *prasad* (offering) and doing *aarti* (prayer) in front of the idol. She would hardly participate in family talks, used to keep *'maun'* (silence) most of the time, and did not interact much with her sons. As a result, they felt neglected and the household work also suffered. Her family repeatedly requested her not to spend so much time worshipping, but her involvement with the Devi increased with each passing day. One day, she was not at home, so the sons in desperation and a fit of anger took the idol to a nearby river and immersed it in the river.

When Raj Kumari came back, she discovered that the idol was missing. She was very upset after hearing what her sons had done. She cried profusely and then withdrew into herself and became quiet. Gradually she lost her appetite, got weak and could hardly sleep. She constantly started fearing that some disaster would happen, and some misfortune would take place, and she and her family would have to suffer now for the bad deed done. Her thoughts were rooted in the belief that the whole family was now doomed since her sons had removed the idol of Devi and immersed it in the river. This thought haunted her. She could not pray, felt restless, experienced heavy breathing, and had severe headaches. She was brought to me in this condition.

The counselling session involved Thought Yoga and Cognitive Restructuring to manage her automatic thoughts and deep-seated schemas, which include beliefs and action patterns developed since childhood. For a few sessions, I made her practice relaxation and taught her relaxation techniques to deal with her anxiety. Immediately after the relaxation session, she felt better and calmer, but this feeling lasted for about one or two days only. After that, her mind went back to her old pattern of thought and the earlier symptoms reoccurred. She again felt restless, anxious, and depressed.

Since her issues were due to a particular religious belief, I decided to make her undergo a special hypnotherapy session which works very well in such cases. Before the session, she was told that by using the power of her mind, she would be able to invoke Goddess Durga and invite courage and happiness into her life. The whole session was conducted in the Hindi language since the client understood that language well.

After relaxing the client and inducing a deep hypnotic trance, the following suggestions were given to her to achieve the desired goal:

"Now that you are relaxed, in this beautiful state of relaxation, you have the power to invoke Goddess Durga and feel Her presence. To invoke Goddess Durga, just visualize Her magnificent form in front of your closed eyes...you can see Her image vividly...now see Her image expanding, growing vaster and bigger, vaster and bigger...and finally enveloping and overpowering your small frame...and merging it into Hers. Let the lion, the manifold hands and all the numerous weapons emerge from YOU! Become YOUR extensions! Her weapons are now YOUR weapons! Centre yourself at the core of Durga! BECOME HER! Feel the strength of Durga inside you. See this with your mind's eyes, making it real!"

"Now hold this vision for some time, till your breath becomes long and deep on its own...and you experience an expansion."

"Now gradually contract her image and bring it to its original size, safely placing this image in your heart. You now dare to meet life in full face...with full force. You are undefeatable, for now, you possess the required boldness to destroy both desire and defeat. You are now fit to face any situation in life anytime, anywhere. Feel the divine power and energy of Goddess Durga in you!"

"You are confident, happy, peaceful, and a positive personality. Your mind is calm and you think positive thoughts. You peacefully accept things you cannot change and you change the things you want to and can change. You experience balance and harmony in your life. You are mentally and physically strong. You have great inner strength. 'Inner Strength' and '*Man ki Shakti*' are your trigger words for post-hypnotic conditioned response."

After repeating these suggestions, the client was brought out of the trance in the prescribed way of hypnotherapy and was brought back to the state of conscious awareness.

Upon awakening, Raj Kumari felt relaxed and calm. She felt as if a unique feeling of peace had descended on her. Her subconscious mind had readily accepted the suggestions and her core belief was reframed. She felt courageous and in control, of herself and her situation. In the follow-up sessions, she reported very little discomfort, and after a few sessions, the therapy was terminated. Raj Kumari now had a unique bond with her Goddess Durga.

"What doesn't kill me, makes me stronger."

- Friedrich Nietzsche

Thought Stopping to Manage Obsessive Compulsive Disorder

Reema, a 21-year-old girl contacted me with her mother. She was the only child in her family and lived away from her hometown to pursue higher studies. She was studying Social Sciences. She was a shy, reserved girl and felt anxious talking to people. For the past four years, she had been suffering from a particular condition. She needed to wash her hands and have a bath every time someone touched her, or if she accidentally touched someone, even her mother. She had divided areas in her house into two sections, pure and impure. Even the sofa in her drawing room had two parts, clean and unclean. She always sat on the clean part of the sofa to feel comfortable. If she sat in any 'impure' part of the house, she had to take a bath. No one in the house was allowed to sit in those parts, or on the sofa which she has labelled as pure. If she went outside, she had to wash her hair, take a bath, and change clothes after returning.

At night, she could not sleep without washing her hair and taking a bath because she had touched many things in her house during the day. Her bed was a 'clean' area. So, how could she sleep on it because she was 'dirty'? This was her daily routine. Sometimes, she would wake up at 3 am, to take a bath and wash her hair. Reema was tired of herself. She realised that she should not be feeling like this and should not behave in this manner, but she was helpless.

Reema continued feeling anxious and disturbed if she did not wash or take a bath. She had beautiful hair, but she had cut it to a smaller length since it was difficult to wash long hair three times a day. She liked to stay alone and had very few friends. Her relationship with her classmates in college was strained because other girls thought she was weird and stayed away from her. She lived alone in a rented room since no one would share a room with her due to her problem.

Reema also stammered if she had to speak in front of unknown people, or in front of her classmates and her teacher. She had consulted a psychiatrist and had taken medicines for one month. She stopped medication since she felt it was not helping her and there was no significant relief in the symptoms. She recalled being abused as a child by one of her cousins and had trust issues as well. Reema's symptoms were suggestive of **Obsessive Compulsive Disorder**, also called **OCD.**

OCD is characterized by the occurrence of unwanted, intrusive, and recurrent obsessive thoughts or distressing images. These are usually accompanied by compulsive behaviours, designed to neutralize obsessive thoughts or images or to prevent a dreaded event or situation. Obsessions involve recurrent and persistent thoughts.

Compulsions involve repetitive behaviours, like hand washing, or mental acts like praying or counting. The affected person feels driven to perform compulsive behaviours in response to an obsession. The behaviour or mental acts are aimed at preventing or reducing anxiety and distress. People with OCD realize that obsessive thoughts and compulsive behaviours are irrational, but they cannot seem to control them. This causes significant distress, consumes excessive time, and interferes with personal, social, and occupational functioning.

Reema was suffering from an obsession of contamination, followed by the compulsive behaviour of washing and cleaning or avoidance of the contaminated object. The skin on her hands had become very rough due to excessive washing. She would suppress her anger and feel depressed most of the time. She was not close to anyone and never shared her issues. She was fond of painting, reading and music.

She recalled that her symptoms first appeared when she was in tenth grade. She was not well and had to be hospitalized for 5 days. She started getting obsessive thoughts of contamination from that time and resorted to washing to feel clean. Reema was visibly disturbed and wanted to resolve her issues.

Her therapeutic intervention included several sessions in which counselling and cognitive restructuring were done. She was asked to practice the 'But' technique and 'Thought Yoga', explained earlier in this book.

An effective technique to manage OCD is **Thought Stopping**.

This was implemented in the following therapy session. Reema was told to close her eyes and vividly imagine a scene which would invoke the thought of being unclean and make her feel the need to wash or take a bath. She was instructed to let me know as soon as she got that thought, by raising her index finger with her eyes still closed. The moment Reema raised her finger, I banged the table hard! **'STOP!'** I exclaimed loudly to jar her out of her thought. Reema instantly opened her eyes, in a state of shock. She slowly realized what had happened and became normal. This was repeated several times in the same session. After a few repetitions, Reema started finding it difficult to have those obsessive thoughts.

Reema was taught to practice thought-stopping outside the therapy session as well. She could bang a table nearby and say 'STOP!' in a loud voice whenever she had the thought of being unclean. The purpose was to distract herself and not give energy to the disturbing thought.

Thoughts are powerless. They have no energy of their own. If we give energy to our thoughts or entertain any thought, it assumes power and disturbs us. After a few sessions of thought-stopping, Reema was told to imagine a placard with 'STOP!' written on it in red colour. The 'STOP!' sign represented danger. Whenever she got an obsessive thought, she had to visualize this sign instructing her to stop the thought immediately.

Reema started practising thought-stopping religiously. She had started learning to manage her thoughts, but sometimes gave in to them too. In addition to thought-stopping, Reema was also counselled to reframe her perception regarding her stay in the hospital. Her treatment was essential, and she would not have recovered if she had not been admitted for her illness. So, she had to think of it as a blessed place which helped her recover to a healthy state. She was also advised to use sanitiser on her hands and change clothes instead of bathing and washing her hair at night before sleeping.

Hypnotherapy and Relaxation techniques were also included in her treatment to deal with the underlying anxiety. Positive suggestions were given after inducing a hypnotic trance, to build confidence and enhance self-esteem. The suggestion "Your mind and body is a car, and YOU are the driver," worked well with her. Under deep hypnosis, Cord Cutting Technique was conducted to help her let go of the traumatic events of her past and set herself free.

Obsessive Compulsive Disorder is very disabling and ego-dystonic (distressing and unacceptable to the ego). Reema reported a 70% relief in her symptoms. Her healing had begun.

While treating symptoms of OCD, psychotherapy can be successfully used as an adjunct to pharmacotherapy if symptoms are severe and the patient is ready to take support of medicines from a psychiatrist.

Hypnodrama to Overcome Fear of Stage Performance

Mandakini, a young 28-year-old singer contacted me to overcome her fear of singing in front of an audience. She was a renowned singer, very well appreciated and had given many performances on stage. A few weeks before she visited me, she had contracted a throat infection with a cold, cough, and fever. She had taken treatment and after recovering, she wanted to resume singing. She somehow started feeling that because of her throat infection, she might not be able to sing as well as she used to before. She did attempt, but a few negative remarks from her colleagues further aggravated her insecurity.

Over time, Mandakini lost all her confidence, was very nervous on stage and felt a lump in her throat whenever she tried to sing. An important event was just a few months away and she had been invited to participate in it. Mandakini was in distress and wanted to overcome this fear that was gripping her. I suggested using Hypnodrama to heal her and she readily agreed.

Hypnodrama is a behaviour modification process used in hypnotherapy. Under hypnotic trance, the hypnotherapist guides the client through an actual event which invokes fear, anxiety and other related issues in the client, due to which the client is not able to perform or cope well during the event.

Hypnodrama is extremely effective in overcoming the fear of public speaking, fear of stage performances, exam anxiety and other such fears. It can also be used to improve sports performance and modify any behaviours that the client wants to change.

Before the actual session, the client was asked to describe the difficult emotions and physical feelings associated with the event. Mandakini shared that every time she had to sing, a lump would form in her throat and she felt afraid that she would not be able to sing. She felt breathless, had sweaty palms and a racing heartbeat. She would resort to overthinking and would be overcome by a nagging feeling that she did not sound good. She also felt that she would be unable to recall the lyrics of the song. The sight of the audience made her feel anxious and nervous. She felt she had no confidence and was a failure.

I asked her what she wanted to feel instead and what qualities she needed the most before her performance. She said she wanted to feel confident, calm, and full of positive thoughts. She wanted to feel abundant positive energy before her performance.

We started the session. After making her feel comfortable and inducing the required state of trance, the following suggestions were given:

"Mandakini, I want you to go back in time, to the time you were feeling very anxious and nervous during the stage performance. Notice all the unpleasant feelings you were experiencing. Notice the lump in your throat, your sweaty hands, heavy breathing, a racing heart, and the feeling of discomfort. Feel all this in its full intensity...and NOW, I will count from 1 to 3. At the count of 3, you will release all these feelings and let them go. Be ready to LET GO!"

"And here it comes.... 1, 2 and 3! Let go of all the discomfort...the lump in your throat has disappeared...your hands are dry and your heartbeat is normal. Now, notice a growing sense of confidence and calmness inside you. You are full of abundant positive thoughts and you feel energetic. Now, allow yourself to travel forward in time, to the day of your next performance.... and notice that you are feeling so confident, calm, and full of positive energy."

"You drink some water and it instantly energizes you. You look at the audience and the sight of the audience relaxes you. As soon as you hold the mic to sing, you feel confident, and you have total recall of the song you want to sing. Whatever little anxiety you are feeling, it motivates you to give your best performance. You notice the melodious music which is playing and you start your performance. You sing your song with much ease and confidence...you can feel the emotion of the song you are singing."

"Notice how your physical body is so relaxed...and you sing with ease, grace and confidence."

"You are halfway through the song now, and you feel happy and calm as you sing, feeling so confident and full of positive energy. You complete the song effortlessly. Singing comes naturally to you. You now put the mic down...you hear the audience breaking into a thunderous applause. You are happy, and there is a beautiful smile on your face. You are a winner who achieves her goals."

When the session ended, Mandakini felt relaxed, confident and in control. She lived in another city about 4 hours away. She used to visit in the morning and leave after the sessions by the evening train for all follow-up sessions. Her dedication to continue therapy and to improve rewarded her with excellent results. She shared that she felt heavenly hearing the thunderous applause after her performance at the event.

To the Reader

In hypnotherapy, anchors or trigger words are used, and they prove to be very effective in achieving the desired response. Any word, symbol, physical act or stimulus can be associated with the desirable body-and-mind response. The anchor or trigger word activates the desirable state and can be used by the client to promote desirable behaviour whenever required.

In this case study, 3 anchors were used:

1) The sight of the audience will relax you.
2) Drinking some water before singing energizes you.
3) As soon as you hold the mic in your hand to sing, you will feel very confident and you will have total recall of the lyrics.

For students facing examination stress and anxiety, the following anchors prove to be very effective:

1) As soon as you enter the examination hall, the sight of the invigilator will relax you.
2) As soon as you fill in the required details in your answer sheet, you will have full confidence.
3) Now that you are relaxed and confident, as soon as you pick up your pen to write the answers, your memory is stimulated and you have total recall.
4) If ever your mind goes blank, put your pen down and when you pick it up again, the recall is there.
5) You are Perfectly Prepared for your exams. **'Perfectly Prepared'** are your trigger words for conditioned response.

Past Life Regression Therapy to Resolve Unexplained Anger

Past life regression therapy or **PLRT** is based on the concept of reincarnation and the belief that many of our present life problems may have their origin in our past life. Though people have diverse views on the subject, reincarnation has been an essential part of Hindu philosophy and has been spoken about in the holy scripture, The Bhagavad Gita.

"vāsānsi jīrṇāni yathā vihāya
navāni gṛihṇāti naro 'parāṇi
tathā śharīrāṇi vihāya jīrṇānya
nyāni sanyāti navāni dehī"

"As a person sheds worn-out garments and wears new ones, likewise, at the time of death, the soul casts off its worn-out body and enters a new one."

- The Bhagavad Gita (Chapter 2, Verse 22)

PLRT is based on the concept that all memories of previous births are stored in the primitive memory of the subconscious mind and can be relived under a deep hypnotic trance. A person can relive the experiences of a past life and describe them as if they are happening in the now. Since hypnosis is a state of dual awareness, a person can alternate between the hypnotic state and the conscious state. Dr. Michael Newton's work on this topic is well depicted in his book 'Journey of Souls.' Dr. Brian Weiss in his book, 'Many Lives, Many Masters,' and in many other books also written by him, has shared extensive data on PLRT through real-life experiences with his clients.

Sujata, a 32-year-old lady contacted me about her major anger issues. She would get upset about little things and would react very badly. Her husband was posted out of India and would visit his family once a year. She lived with her two children, a son and a daughter, and her mother-in-law. Her relationship with her mother-in-law was extremely strained. There were constant arguments and disagreements on petty matters. Sujata was career oriented, but unable to pursue a professional life. She approached me for counselling to deal with her anger issues.

A couple of relaxation sessions later, she did feel composed and relaxed for one or two days, but her anger kept resurfacing on petty issues. Counselling gives relief for some time, but the mind tends to go back to the old pattern of thought, especially in deep-rooted issues. One day, she approached me, very hassled, and reported that in a fit of anger, she had hit her TV with a bat and the TV was reduced to pieces. She also confessed that she had bought a dagger from somewhere and was constantly plagued by thoughts of attacking herself or the object of her rage. A little probing revealed that her anger was mostly directed towards her mother-in-law.

Sujata was visibly disturbed. She expressed a desire to undergo Past Life Regression Therapy. She felt that maybe it had the answers to her present state since she was shocked and in disbelief of her own behaviour. I agreed and we decided to proceed with it.

During the PLRT, under a deep hypnotic trance, she regressed to a past life where she was a male. In response to appropriate suggestions, Sujata started talking...

"I am a dacoit and a male. I am wearing black clothes. I have long hair and an elongated black tilak on my forehead. I am married and I have two children. I am the head of my clan. I am very aggressive. I am involved in looting and killings. It is a remote area in Rajasthan where we live. The sand is red here."

On probing further as to who was the most important person in her life in that lifetime, she revealed:

"The most important person in my life is my mother. She keeps coaxing me to get as much money as possible, in whatever way I can. My whole life is engaged in killings, looting, and bringing money home."

I probed further and asked her if she had any connection with her mother in the present lifetime, and whether she recognized her in the present lifetime. She replied, *"Yes, she is my mother-in-law in my present life."*

Sujata could vividly recall the voices of horses, the sounds of hooves, the names of other dacoits in her clan, and the rivers and bridges they used to cross during their loot expeditions. She recalled the exact year as well, it was 1819. Her entire life was spent like this, in brutal attacks, lootings, and killings. In one such attack, Sujata gets hit by a bullet. She dies and the spirit leaves the body.

The All-Knowing Spirit revealed that the purpose of that life was the realization that anger is futile and there is no need to kill. It is not required. Life must be lived peacefully. She could not learn it in that lifetime, so she was still suffering and carrying that anger within herself, in her present life. I requested her Higher Self to help her let go of her anger and realize the purpose of her life.

I then terminated the session and brought her back to the present and out of the deep hypnotic trance. Sujata was full of sweat and visibly shaken. I asked her to share her experience. She took a while and gradually came back to her normal self, this time subdued. Though she seemed shaken, there was an uncanny calm on her face.

Slowly, taking her time, she revealed that she remembered everything of that lifetime and got her answers as to why she experienced so much anger. She had been carrying it for lifetimes without knowing any plausible reason. She looked calm, and composed and had a peaceful sense of knowing. There was silence and a long pause. After the heavy silence, I could make out that she was ready to talk. I asked her "How do you feel now?"

"I'm feeling...overwhelmed," she replied in a calm voice.

I said to her, "I think, now the anger and your relationship with your mother-in-law will also improve."

Sujata's reply was a wonderful revelation, "What's there to be angry about? She has all the right to scold me...even slap me. After all, she is my mother."

In that moment, I was amazed at the power of PLRT and the potential it has to reveal answers, change perceptions and heal lifetimes of trauma. Sujata continues to meet me. Her relationships have improved and she is pursuing a career of her choice.

The ability to love and the ability to forgive, are the weapons God has given us to live in this not so perfect world.

Past Life Regression Therapy to Understand and Resolve Unexplained Body Pain

Rani contacted me to learn about hypnotherapy. She had read about hypnosis and self-hypnosis. She was interested in the course and wanted to learn it to help herself and others. She is a pretty lady, 37 years old, and usually wears graceful flowing dresses.

During the course, she shared that she suffered from continuous body pain. All parts of her body felt like they were under constant stress. She often felt uneasy and experienced discomfort. Rani had learned to live with the pain. She had consulted many doctors and had all the required tests done. All her reports were normal and the doctors could not diagnose any ailment.

After she completed the workshop on Hypnotherapy, she got quite interested in the subject and expressed her desire to undergo Past Life Regression Therapy to find out the cause of her unexplained body pain. A day of mutual convenience was decided and we started the session.

***We never close our eyes. We only close our eyelids. When we close our eyelids, our eyes open to our beautiful inner world.**￼*

Under deep hypnosis, I suggested to her subconscious mind to select and go to that relevant past life which would reveal the answers to her present problems. Under hypnosis, it is possible to access the deep-seated information buried in the primitive memory of the subconscious mind.

Rani regressed to a life many years back, in the 18th century. She is 19 years old. She is in India and she belongs to a royal family. She wears beautiful flowing dresses like lehengas and heavy saris. She wears lots of jewellery and loves to dress up. Her hair is adorned with beautiful jasmine flowers. She has many maids to look after her every need. She is the only daughter of her parents and lives happily.

Rani is in love with a boy named Ramakant. She is afraid to tell this to her parents as she feels that they will not approve of the relationship. She meets Ramakant secretly whenever she can. He also loves her. She has a close friend with whom she has shared about Ramakant. They wanted to get married but were afraid to reveal that to her parents. Rani recognized Ramakant as her husband in her present life.

I guided her to move forward in that lifetime to a significant event in that life and describe what she saw.

She is at the local fair. There are thousands of people around her. Ramakant is also there. They had planned to meet at the fair. Rani had confided in her friend that she would be going to the fair and so, her friend had arranged their meeting. Her friend is also with her. They are having a good time. She is enjoying herself. Suddenly, there is a loud bang, like the sound of a gunshot. Rani was not sure what happened. She just heard the loud noise and then heard people screaming and everyone was running helter-skelter. There was total confusion and chaos. Suddenly, someone pushed her and she fell down. She could not see her friend Ramakant in the commotion. In no time, it all turned into a stampede. Rani could feel many people stepping over her body and running away. She was badly hurt and bruised all over. She tried to get up but could not, with people constantly stomping her down. Ultimately, Rani's physical body could no longer take the brutal assault and she died. The spirit left the body.

While narrating this, Rani showed signs of immense physical distress and discomfort. I gave her suggestions to disconnect from all the trauma and release the pain, release the emotions connected with that lifetime, and feel free.

I brought her out of that state to the present life, back to conscious awareness. Rani felt relaxed and relieved. She could recall everything she had seen, and the reason for her unexplained body pain.

She was happy to be connected to Ramakant in the present life too. Rani shared that she realized that you are never separated from your loved ones, and you can spend lifetimes together. This insight also brought a huge sense of relief to her.

She came again for a follow-up session. Rani's body pain was healed.

"Journey into the beautiful dream that is life...the end is only the beginning."

- Dr. Brian L. Weiss

SUGGESTION IS POWER

I was at the Delhi airport waiting for the boarding announcement for Bhopal. There was still time for the boarding to start. I settled down in a chair and glanced all around. I noticed a young man dressed formally in a suit, sitting opposite, a little far away. He looked engrossed in his laptop, typing endlessly. I relaxed in my seat, took out my mobile and started reading my emails.

After some time, suddenly I heard someone call my name, "Ritu Ma'am, Ritu Ma'am." I looked up and was surprised to see that young man kneeling beside me, trying to grab my attention. I was taken aback. "Ritu Ma'am! Did you recognize me?" he asked. As I looked closely at him, recognition dawned and with it a pleasant surprise. "Oh, are you Aditya?" I asked knowingly.

He nodded. Without waiting for his reply, I continued in an elated tone, "You were pursuing the BPT (Bachelor of Physiotherapy) course and I taught you Psychology in your first year! You used to write the best answers!" "Yes Ma'am," he replied with a smile, "Ma'am, do you remember you used to tell me after every class, 'Aditya, why are you doing BPT? You deserve to be a doctor; you have the mindset and the skills.' Your words would linger in my mind long after. Ma'am, before joining the BPT course, I had taken the entrance exam for Medicine, but could not clear it. That's why I had decided to do the Bachelor of Physiotherapy course. But your constant words of motivation made me think again. I took another chance to get entrance into a medical college. My efforts paid off. Today I am a doctor."

I kept looking at him with joy and surprise and my heart swelled with a beautiful feeling of happiness and fulfilment. He continued, "Right now I'm going for my first job. I can't thank you enough Ma'am. Keep blessing me."

I thanked Aditya for remembering me and blessed him. Soon, the boarding started. I kept wondering how the power of continued suggestions can change mindsets and lives. This memory is deeply etched in my mind and many such instances are my true rewards.

GRATITUDE TO ALL

This is what fuels me to wake up each morning and give The Beautiful Universe my All.

"Thank you Ritu, for such an energising, empowering, healing session. I am grateful to you for allowing me to be a part of this space. Look forward to more."

Lina Parasuram
Life Coach, Yoga Teacher & Fitness Coach - Lifestyle Wellness Solutions

"Such an enriching and enlightening session. Ritu Ma'am gave in-depth knowledge with excellent real-life examples that were so easy to understand and relate to. A complete eye opener."

Pooja Sood
ESL Trainer, Mississauga Sec. Academy - Ontario, Canada

"Thank you very much Ritu Ma'am for such wonderful session, it wasn't only learning about hypnosis, I am feeling enlightenment after a long time. Thanks for uplifting our confidence and emotional state."

Kalpana Verma

"Thank you so much for such an enlightening session. I was a parent participant and could understand the techniques quite well... extremely good explanation by Ritu Ma'am."

Participant
Parent - New Delhi

"The Power of Subconscious Mind - By the renowned psychologist #DrRituNanda. Highly Qualified, Knowledgeable, Experienced, Witty and Absolutely Adorable!! Unmissable!!

#BlockYourCalendar #EverythingElseCanWait"

Rajeev Mishra
Soft Skills Coach, Talk Show Host

"Ritu Ma'am, thank you so much for the awesome learning session. Enjoyed a lot. Loved it!"

Shubhanka Kala
Senior Neuro Psychologist - Jaipur

"My heartfelt thanks, I'm filled with gratitude Ma'am, such an inspiring and insightful session. Looking forward for more such sessions. As soon as the session started, we all were in trance. Thanks for the mesmerising session."

Anushree Agrawal
Faculty, Sagar Public School - Bhopal

"Thank you Ritu Ma'am for such an enriching and excellent workshop...It's always such a pleasure to attend workshops under you. May I have more such opportunities."

Richa Dubey
Psychologist, Retd. Airforce Officer - Karnataka

"Dear Ma'am, thanks a lot for a knowledge filled workshop. Really very helpful to deal with children and adults. You explained things in a very simple manner. Look forward to this kind of workshop in future."

Shraddha Dubey
Faculty - Art of Living

"Wonderful webinar. Ma'am session was too too good. Your way of explanation...and with every point you gave examples. Very easy to understand. Really very nice."

Heminder Kaur
Special Educator - Mohali, Punjab

"My heartfelt thanks, I'm filled with gratitude. Such an inspiring and insightful session."

Dipika
Counsellor

"Thank you so much Ritu Ma'am for such an amazing session. In these two days, I learned so many new techniques and now I have started loving hypnotherapy. Once again, thank you for giving me such a wonderful opportunity."

Pankhuri Agrawal
Student, B.A. (Hons.), Psychology

"Thanks a lot Ritu Ma'am for this wonderful and extensive session, learnt a lot. You have comprehended so well this hypnosis topic."

Prabhjot
Entrepreneur & Reiki Practitioner - Pune

"Such an insightful session...I am a counselling psychologist but feel there is so much more to learn and understand about human behaviour. It was indeed a great learning experience. Looking forward to more such rewarding experiences."

Dr. Ritu Bhasin Dhawan
Counselling Psychologist - New Delhi

"Wonderful session Ma'am, as usual. I love your sessions as I understand so well. You have answered, with examples, all our queries. So many takeaways. Gratitude."

Nandita G. Sarma
Faculty & Counsellor - Delhi Public School, Assam

"Excellent session Ritu Ma'am. We never think of reinforcement and stimulus whenever a desired or undesired behaviour occurs. From now on, we will be very observant. Thank you very much."

Purnima Jairam
Participant

"Thank you so much Madam. Great session. Without even wasting a single second, you shared a lot of information. Really feel blessed to get you as our Guru, who lit our hearts to the world of hypnosis."

Binesh K. Menon
Principal, Counsellor & Trainer - Kerala

"Your session had a great impact on me. I am surrounded with positive aura emitted by you even now. Thank you Ma'am."

Nandita G. Sarma
Faculty & Counsellor - Delhi Public School, Assam

Celebrate life!

ABOUT THE AUTHOR

Dr. Ritu has conducted extensive workshops, seminars and training programs for Dire Dawa University (Ethiopia, Africa), LIC Housing Finance Ltd., Centre for Research and Industrial Staff Performance (CRISP), Bharat Heavy Electricals Limited (BHEL), National Judicial

Academy, National Insurance Company, TATA Teleservices Ltd, Indian Coast Guards, State Crime Record Bureau (SCRB), NIT Hamirpur (Himachal Pradesh), Central Bank Officers Training Centre (CBOTC), Central Power Research Industry (CPRI), Sports Authority of India (Ministry of Youth Affairs & Sports, Government of India), District Karate Association, National AIDS Control Organization (NACO), Rajiv Gandhi National Ground Water Training and Research Institute, National Institute of Fashion Technology (NIFT), All India Institute of Medical Sciences (AIIMS), Bhopal School of Social Sciences (BSSS), Delhi Public School, Sagar Group of Institutions, Bhopal (Schools & Engineering Colleges), Jagran Lake City University, Ambuja Group of Schools and various other prestigious institutions of education.

Dr. Ritu was invited as a resource person at the 9th National Conference of Hypnotherapy at Jawaharlal Nehru University, New Delhi. She has presented papers on varied topics at National and International Conferences in Bangalore, Pune, Delhi, Mumbai, Agra, Bhopal, Indore, and Vadodara. She has been a guest speaker on mental health, hypnotherapy, and social issues with FM, Prasar Bharti, Doordarshan and Private Television Channels.

Besides the workshops and training programs, Dr. Ritu provides Individual Counselling to clients across India, USA, Paris and Singapore.

Let's heal together.

Each one of us can make a difference.
Together we make change.

Get in touch with **Dr. Ritu Nanda**.

Website: www.drritunanda.com

Email: drritunanda@gmail.com

LinkedIn: www.linkedin.com/in/drritunanda

9 798889 415052 9